Jesus' Resurrection

Our Inheritance

Dr. Donald A. Peart

Jesus' Resurrection, Our Inheritance
Copyright © 2012 Donald A. Peart

Cover design by Jeshua Peart

All emphasis in the references is supplied by the author. Please note that the King James Version with "old English" spelling is one of the Bible versions used in this book, unless otherwise noted. In some references from the King James Version, some corrections to match the modern spelling have been made.

Edition: September 2022

ISBN: 978-0-9852481-1-6

Acknowledgments

It seemed good to our Father, the Father of our Lord Jesus Christ, who desired to have these things written. Thanks to our heavenly Father for your Holy Spirit who teaches and directs us.

Thanks to Judith, the wife of my youth who belongs to Christ; and I also acknowledge our children (Donald Jr., Jeshua, Charity, Benjamin, and Jesse) who also have been baptized by His Holy Spirit into Christ, Jesus.

Thanks to Crown of Glory Ministries (a Church of our Lord Jesus Christ) that we founded and currently oversee; and they I also believe belong to the Lord Jesus Christ.

Table of Contents

The Resurrections

Resurrection is defined as "the act of rising from the dead." The Greek word used for resurrection in the Bible means "to stand up again." **Everyone** that has died or will die, God[1] will raise them from the dead. **All** will "stand up again."

Resurrection is a fact that is "assumed [taken for granted] in the Scriptures."[2] That is, God does not have to prove to anyone the reality of resurrection; even though, there are many who do not believe in the resurrection from the dead. The Scriptures appear to indicate that there are basically four[3] resurrections, each resurrection consisting of <u>at least</u> two phases.

<u>First:</u> There is the resurrection of Jesus, Himself.[4] Jesus' resurrection occurred approximately two thousand years ago. <u>Second:</u> There will be a resurrection the Bible calls the resurrection of the "the firstfruit Christ," a resurrection that I consider one of the phases "the first resurrection."[5] <u>Third</u>: There will be the resurrection of "those who are Christ's at His coming,"[6] the other phase of the first resurrection.

<u>Fourth:</u> There is also the resurrection of what I call the "finish" or "conclusion."[7] The resurrection at the "finish" or "conclusion" appears to be synonymous with the "resurrection … of eternal judgment."[8] At the resurrection of eternal judgment **"all"** the "rest of the dead" who were not raised, permanently, in the previous resurrections will be raised from the dead.[9] With that said, let us look a more closely at each of the four resurrections listed above.

The Resurrection of Jesus

Jesus' resurrection is the **pattern** for the other resurrections. The resurrection of Jesus Christ was the "firstfruit" resurrection. Jesus' resurrection was the "first" of "many ... Saints" who would also to be raised permanently from the dead. Jesus' resurrection consisted of two phases. Jesus Himself being raised from the dead was the first phase; and the second phase consists of the "many bodies of the Saints" that were also resurrected just "after" Jesus was raised from the dead.[10]

There is also a difference between "life" and "resurrection." The resurrection is an event in time, and the resurrection is also a Person. Jesus declared the resurrection to be a Person (Jesus, Himself), **and** an event in time. Jesus also declared Himself to be "the life." Jesus Himself defines "the life" to mean that if a believer in Christ has faith "into" Jesus, he or she does not ever have to die.

John 11:25-26: [25]*Jesus said unto her,* **I am the resurrection, and the life:** *he that believe in (lit., into) me, though he were dead, yet shall he live:* [26]*And whosoever lives and believe in (lit., into) me shall never die. Believe you this?*

"Resurrection" and "the Life" is personified in Jesus when Jesus said that "**I am** the resurrection **and** the life." Thus, resurrection is not just an event. **Resurrection is foremost a Person—Jesus.** This can mean that if you have Jesus in you, then you have the resurrection in you! "The Life" is also a Person. Jesus said, "Search the scriptures; for in them you think you have eternal **life:** and they are they which testify of me. And you will not **come to me,** that you might have **life.**"[11]

The Scripture testifies of Jesus and His resurrection (eternal) life; and this "life" or "eternal life" is not "the Scriptures" as some may "think." The Scriptures do indeed witness of Jesus' resurrection, as we will see a little later in this book. However, the Scriptures also lead you to a **Person—Jesus.** One must **"come"** to **the Person (Jesus)** who is "eternal life." Saying it another way, studying is not enough; one must "come" to Jesus in prayer and relationship.

There was a time in my life when studying the Scripture was my focus. I often studied longer than I would pray. The Lord Jesus has graced me to have studied for up to eight hours straight. The Lord Jesus has also energized me to pray to God, the Father through the night.

We must be able to consistently pray for durations to maintain the balance between knowing the Scriptures and coming to God in prayer. Allow me to tell you an event. Early one morning, around three o'clock, I got up to spend time with the Lord Jesus. As I opened the Scripture to read rather than getting on my knees to pray, **I heard the audible voice of the Lord behind me say, "He is not here, He is risen!"** [12]

The Lord was saying to me "[the] risen" Jesus is not "here" (in the "letter" of the Scriptures) I was reading. God wanted me to first seek the living Person of the "risen" One—Jesus, then study (We are indeed called to know[13] the Scriptures). The Scriptures teaches us to "come" to the Jesus, the Christ, who is "risen." Jesus is the resurrection! The Scripture points to a resurrected Person. This Person (Jesus) is the Life, and He is the resurrection, since **"he is risen, as He said.**[14]

Therefore, if we believe "into" Jesus, we will eventually **"be"** sons of the resurrection.[15] Jesus is indeed the resurrection; and according to the Scripture, resurrection will also become our **"being."** Yet, resurrection is also an event in time.

"In the [event of] resurrection," there will be no marriages.[16] "The resurrection" is "'**in'** the last day."[17] The last day is also an event in time. This "last day" can be understood to mean the last one thousand years, counting the years from the fall of Adam. "One day is with the Lord as a thousand years and a thousand years as one day."[18] Thus, the last **day**, is the last **thousand years** if one starts counting the years from the fall of the **first Adam.**[19]

Jesus is the last Adam.[20] Thus, if we look at the last day from Jesus' time, using Peter's day-years principle, we are at the commencement of the third thousand years from when Jesus came in the flesh. Or we are three days from when Jesus Christ was manifested in the flesh. The prophet Hosea, in Hosea 6:2, was also given a glimpse of the resurrection according to Peter's year-day principle.

*Hosea 6:2: After **two days** will he **revive** us: **in the third day** he will **raise** us up, and **we shall live in his sight.***

This can be interpreted to mean that "two days," or two thousand years from Jesus' resurrection must be completed first; **then,** "in the third day" God will resurrect those who will have **"course"**[21] in the first resurrection "and **we** will live in His sight."

We who "live in His sight" will be resurrected in phases, or by courses, or by ranks. I repeat, in the resurrections there are courses (different phases) and an order (rank) of resurrections.[22] Jesus' resurrection was the pattern that shows the two phases and rank in the resurrections to come.

The preeminent "rank" in the resurrections is the resurrection of Jesus—"Christ is risen out of the dead ones and became the firstfruit of them that have been put to sleep."[23] Jesus was the first to be permanently raised from the dead.[24] The next in line and rank soon after Jesus' resurrection is the revitalization of **"many** of the bodies of the saints which slept."[25] The saints who were raised from sleep immediately after Jesus' resurrection make up the second phase of Jesus' pattern of resurrection. Note: it was not "all" of the bodies of the saints that were raised. It was **"many"** of them.

These "many" were resurrected **after** Jesus was raised from the dead. The truth that there are two courses (phases) in Jesus' resurrection is important to know; because it first establishes Jesus' resurrection as the "first-rank" of all to be raised from the dead. Secondly, His resurrection is also **the pattern.** With this knowledge, it follows that **the subsequent resurrections appear to also have at least two phases in them, except for the resurrection of the firstfruit Christ which seems to have an overlapping phase with the first resurrection.**

Again, for clarity, Jesus' resurrection had two courses (phases). Jesus was the first rank and first phase; because as the Scriptures say, "in all things He might have the preeminence."[26] The second phase after Jesus' resurrection was the "many" saints who were also raised from the dead. Because Jesus' resurrection is the pattern, which has two phases; it follows that in the first resurrection, there will also be at least two "courses" (or phases), or at least two orders. This is seen in 1 Corinthians 15:23 and Revelation 20:4-5.

The Resurrection of the Firstfruit Christ

The resurrection of the "firstfruit Christ" is different from those who will be raised at Jesus' coming; even though it seems that the resurrection in the coming of the Lord is one of the **"courses"** of the first resurrection.

The firstfruit Christ, includes, but is not limited to those[27] who will be the first to become just like Jesus in character, around the completion of this age. The firstfruit Christ will be full of the spirit of prophesy, the testimony of Jesus. They will also experience martyrdom like Jesus; people will be happy the firstfruit Christ were killed, like some wickedly rejoice over the death of Jesus, and these "firstfruit Christ" will be resurrected soon after their apparent death like Jesus was resurrected in short order.

Like Jesus, they will also be the first to **corporately** experience resurrection out of the dead **for people to see**. This resurrection will bring repentance to some. **The second course of the firstfruit resurrection** is the other course(s) in the first resurrection of the **"blessed and holy"** ones. All who are raised in the first resurrection will rule <u>with</u> Christ for a thousand years with resurrected bodies as John declared in Revelation 20:4. **Note:** I believe the first resurrection overlaps two phases. The first resurrection is part of the phase of the firstfruit Christ, because the firstfruit Christ is the **first (beginning fruit)** of the first resurrection. The first resurrection is also a phase of the coming of the Lord; because in His coming, the rest of the dead in Christ will be **first to rise.**

The First Resurrection

The third resurrection, in order, according to Paul, will be the resurrection of those who are Christ's at His coming. That is, those who belong to Jesus Christ will be raised from the dead, **first, "the dead in Christ shall rise first."** This makes the coming of the Lord synonymous with the **"first resurrection"** in the book of Revelation. This resurrection also includes the "change" of the living believer "in Christ" that has been sealed, is being sealed and shall be sealed with the Holy Spirit, because of their trust that Jesus is the Christ. They will be changed, and made incorruptible, immortal, etcetera. This appears to be the second phase of the resurrection in His coming. Thus, like the resurrection of Jesus, there are also two phases in the resurrection at His coming ("the dead in Christ shall rise first;" and then, the living shall be changed thereupon).

The Resurrection of Eternal Judgment

The fourth resurrection in order is the **"resurrection ... of eternal judgment;"**[28] which Paul called "the end" resurrection in 1 Corinthians 15:20-24a. (Note: Paul's topic in 1 Corinthians 15:20-24 is resurrection—Christ, the firstfruit, the firstfruit Christ, they that are Christ's at His coming and finally "the end" resurrection). This "end" resurrection also has two phases.

In this resurrection "all" of the dead that were not "separated" out to participate in the previous resurrections will be raised. In this resurrection it appears to me that there will be two groups judged by their works. Those who **"have done**[29] **(produced or authored) good"** will be resurrected unto life. Those who have **"habitually practiced,"** evil will be "resurrected unto 'crisis'."

In this resurrection, the eternal judgment, which will be good for some and bad[30] for some, will be determined by Him who sits on the Great White Throne. In this resurrection of eternal judgment, those who are <u>not</u> written in the Book of Life will experience the second death—the lake of fire for ages upon ages.

However, I believe there will also be grace and mercy during this eternal judgment. That is, there appears to be resurrection unto life for those who have "produced 'good'." In other words, in the resurrection of eternal judgment if any is found written in the Book of Life they will be saved.

This is understood because the Scripture does not explicitly say that all the dead that are raised in the resurrection of eternal judgment will experience the second death. The

Scripture says, that **"if any"** was not found written in the Book of Life; then they would be punished. Jesus also said some will be resurrected unto to life at that time when **"all"** who are in the graves will hear His voice.[31]

Thus, one of the purposes of this book is to encourage believers who are already Christ's (those already baptized into Christ through the Holy Spirit) to be careful to maintain "good works"[32] by the Holy Spirit with a view to be partakers of their inheritance in the resurrection of the dead. Another purpose is that those who do not currently have Jesus as their Lord may make Him Lord of their lives by going beyond what the Bible calls the "common salvation" into the "great salvation," and into the "eternal salvation," being sealed by the Holy Spirit of promise.

With all that was said above, I am careful in my writing to remain Scriptural, remembering the nails of the cross that also shed Jesus' blood, because of a vision the Lord gave me concerning writing.

On February 26, 2005, I saw in a vision an elderly man with white hair, white beard, clothed in white. (I am not sure[33] if this man was the Ancient of days, or the beloved John?) The man had a writer's pen (nail) in his hand. I saw the pen being held up and inspected by this man. The pen was sharp (pointy) with what appeared to be blood-like ink on its point. I had the impression that the pen was a nail of the cross. I then heard a voice say, that "John (the beloved apostle) was more honorable than they, because he wrote with the nail of a cross."

In the vision I was dressed liked a young Jew (Romans 2:28-29), with a priestly turban on my head. The elderly man with white robe, the white hair, the white beard also had tears of blood flowing from his eyes. In the vision, I kept observing the aged man, as he observed the nail with the ink of blood on its tip.

Thus, I am inclined to say, I am but a man writing with limited understanding through the blood of Jesus; as Job explained, we understand only "parts (edges) of His ways."[34] God, who stretched the north over an empty place,[35] who among us knows how? God, who hung the earth on nothing,[36] again, who among us knows how? God, who can bind water in clouds,[37] the pillars of heaven tremble at His correction,[38] what can we say to this truth? God, who divides the sea, God, who smites Rahab[39] (a dragon in the sea); God, who brightens the heavens,[40] the thunder of God's power who can understand?[41]

It is the same in regards to understanding His eternal power and times of resurrections. The resurrections are only understood fully by the Father, the Son, and the Holy Spirit. We only know "the edges" of His intent relative to the resurrections; and it appears that God left some times and season obscure,[42] purposely! So, if I have overlooked some things in this book, please do not throw words of stones. Paul indicated that The Lord Jesus alone shall show in "His own seasons" who is the only Dynasty, "The King of kings and the Lord of lords!"

Blessings,
Donald Peart, "called to be a son"

Jesus' Resurrection, the Pattern

*1 Corinthians 15:19-22: [19]If in this life only we have **hope** in Christ, we are of all men most miserable. [20]But now is Christ risen from the dead and become the **firstfruit**[43] **of them that slept.** [21]For since **by man** came death, **by man** also came the resurrection of the dead. [22]For as in Adam all die, even so in Christ shall all be made alive.*

Jesus Christ and we (His saints) becoming like Him is a facet of our hope.[44] There appears to be a lot of **misery** in the world because most have no real hope for life after "this life." Paul stated in the text above that because of Jesus' resurrection there is "hope" for us beyond "this life only." Thus, **"now is Christ risen from the dead"** and has given us hope.

This is the hope: as Jesus Christ is the first to be risen from the dead never to experience death again, He has provided the same opportunity to all humanity, especially those who belong to Jesus Christ. Thus, "they that are Christ's" will also be resurrected or will put on immortality in the "seventh trumpet," which is the same as the "last trumpet."

*1 Peter 1:3, NKJ: Blessed be the God and Father of our Lord Jesus Christ, who according to His abundant mercy has begotten us again to a living **hope** through the **resurrection of Jesus** Christ from the dead.*

Jesus is the "firstfruit" of the resurrections; "Now is Christ risen from the dead and become the **firstfruit** of them that slept. For since by man [Adam] came death, by man [Jesus, the last Adam] also came resurrection of the dead."

The first Adam (Mr. and Mrs. Adam) was the firstfruit of death—the first humans to experience death. Conversely, the last Adam (Jesus) is the firstfruit of the resurrection. Mr. and Mrs. Adam were the catalyst by which all humans outside of Christ are still subject to die.

So likewise, Jesus Christ is the first to experience resurrection life, so that those who are His seed are predetermined to be made alive in Him. There is no doubt that death is passed to humans by **one man,** Adam. This is seen in the fact that mankind in general is still dying.

Conversely, Jesus has also passed on His very life to those who are in Christ. That is, we are no longer subject to sin and death. We do not have to die any more. Why? "For as in Adam all die, **even so** <u>in Christ shall **all** be made alive.</u>"

Mankind in general does not choose to die. Death comes as a part of living, and because God's ways are equal, we can now live without death (dying) by Jesus' gift to us. As death passed down from Adam without choice, so life, as a gift, is imparted to those who believe in Jesus Christ.[45] Believers **do not have to die.** Jesus Himself said, "I am the resurrection, and the life … **whosoever lives and believes in me shall never die.** Believe you this?"[46]

All we need to do is believe "into" the resurrection **and** the life of Jesus. A person being resurrected is different from a person who believes into the "life" of Jesus. "Whosoever **lives** and **believes in [Jesus] shall never die.**"

Jesus is the first person to conquer death completely — He is "the life." He also said that we can do the same as He did; we can conquer death in this life. What we must do is "believe 'into'" Him, and we "shall never die." The thing that we need is the same thing people lacked in the days when Jesus walked the earth in the flesh; we need "trust."

Yet there is mercy for us (some) who apparently lack the faith to "never die." If we do not have the "faith" to conquer death in this life, God has made a way for us to be resurrected through Jesus, anyway. Remember, Jesus said, "I am the resurrection…**though he may die, he shall live."**[47] This truth provides hope in His everlasting mercy!

Thus, it must be through "the Man" (Jesus) that the **expectation** of resurrection is imparted to all. We do not have to die; and if we do die, we will be raised again **through Jesus.** And as for those who do not believe in Christ, there is still a resurrection for them, the resurrection of eternal judgment, whether they believe in resurrections or not.

Why potentially live in misery at the resurrection of eternal judgment by not believing the Scriptures concerning Jesus' resurrection? His resurrection has benefits in this life and the life to come. Why be in misery in Death and Hades after physical death by not receiving the record that Jesus' justification is available to all mankind through His cross and His resurrection?

He rose again from the dead for you and me to have eternal life[48]. He did this approximately two thousand years ago, according to the Scriptures; and according to Scriptures, men have seen Him in His resurrected state as a witness to us of this life in Jesus.

Jesus' Resurrection According to the Scriptures

---

1 Corinthians 15:3-4: *[3]For I delivered unto you first of all that which I also received, how that Christ died for our sins **according to the Scriptures;** [4]And that he was buried, and that he rose again the third day **according to the Scriptures.***

The witness of the Scriptures testifies that Christ was raised from the dead permanently. The Scriptures provided a "surer"[49]basis that stabilizes the expectation of the saints with respect to the guarantee of resurrection. Resurrection is **"according to the Scriptures."**

Paul made this statement in the New Testament. Thus, the "Scriptures" Paul was referencing must have come from the Old Testament (the New Testament was not formulated at the time that Paul cited his "Scripture" references). Isaiah was one of the Old Testament prophets to speak of resurrection.

Isaiah declared that "your dead men shall live, together with my dead body shall they arise."[50] Job also declared resurrection.[51] Jesus Himself also followed the pattern of quoting the Old Testament (i.e., the book of Jonah) with respect to the surety of His resurrection.

*Matthew 12:40: For **as Jonas** was **three days** and **three nights** in the whale's belly; so, shall the **Son of man** be **three days** and **three nights** in the heart of the earth.*

*John 2:19; 21: [19]Jesus answered and said unto them, destroy this temple, and in **three days** I will raise it up... [21]But he spoke of the temple of his body.*

Jesus was "in the heart of the earth" three days and three nights, "according to the Scriptures." He raised "the temple of His Body" in three days as He promised. The Scriptures of Jonah was one of Jesus' authorities relative to Jesus' resurrection in three days.

Jesus, Himself said that "the Scriptures cannot be broken."[52] Thus, all things that the Scripture states will happen must materialize. Jesus also stated that heaven and earth will pass away, but His words will not pass away until all is fulfilled. This is true for the prophetic Scriptures of Jonah.

*Jonah 1:17: Now the LORD had prepared a great fish to swallow up Jonah. **And Jonah was in the belly of the fish three days and three nights.***

For those who do not know the history of Jonah, God sent Jonah to preach to Nineveh. Jonah refused to preach and ran from God. He eventually ended up in a ship and was thrown off the same ship after it was concluded by the sailors that the ship ended up in a storm because of Jonah's disobedience.

A whale swallowed Jonah; and after three days and three nights in the whale's belly, Jonah reconsidered and prayed for deliverance. The whale eventually vomited Jonah; and Jonah went and preached to Nineveh as the Lord originally directed him.

Jesus indicated that Jonah's experience in the whale's belly also pointed to the experience that Jesus would experience "in the heart of the earth." Except that **it was not** because of Jesus' disobedience that Jesus went to the heart of the earth, but because of mankind's sins, Jesus died for us. This same Jesus was also raised out of the heart of the earth for our justification. Without resurrection there is no justification, according to the Scriptures.

Jesus "was delivered for our offenses and was **raised again for our justification.**"[53] This "justification (lit., righteousness)" was also according to the Scriptures of Daniel, Isaiah, and so on. Jesus, the Messiah, did **"bring in everlasting righteousness ...."**[54] "By His knowledge shall my righteous servant **justify many;** for He shall bear their iniquities."[55]

As can be seen, Jesus Himself also used the Scripture as an authority with respect to declaring His resurrection after three days. Peter said that the prophetic word of God is the "more sure word."[56] Jesus knew the surety of the Scripture. He was the living Word walking among them; and He is the living Word in us.[57] The Jews also had an understanding concerning the surety of the Scriptures.

Thus, Jesus' use of the Scriptures concerning His resurrection in three days and nights was so potent that the Jews went through great lengths to attempt to prevent it by human's means. They attempted to label His resurrection a "deception," before Jesus was raised from the dead.

Again, why were they so preoccupied with the "third day" resurrection? The answer is the Pharisees knew the Scriptures. They knew the surety of the fulfillment of the Scriptures. To prove my point, they were more caught up in searching the Scriptures, rather than seeking the One who wrote the Scriptures.[58]

Matthew 27:62-64, NIV: [62]*The **next day,** the one after Preparation Day, **the chief priests and the Pharisees** went to Pilate.* [63]*"Sir," they said, "we remember that while he was still alive that deceiver said, '**After three days I will rise again.'** [64]So give the order for the tomb to be made secure until the third day. Otherwise, his disciples may come and steal the body and tell the people that he has been raised from the dead. This last **deception** will be worse than the first."*

The chief priests and the Pharisees knew the Scriptures. They knew the surety of the Word of God being fulfilled. Thus, they tried to label Jesus' resurrection a "deception" before it happened. The high priest of that day also had a personal vendetta against Jesus. History tells us that when Jesus sacked the merchandisers in the temple for the merchandising sheep, ox, and doves in the temple, He sacked the high priest's profitable business.

According to the Scriptures, the Pharisees' were also jealous of Jesus' popularity. They knew He is the Son of God, and they knew He is the "Heir,"[59] which were reasons they wanted to deny His resurrection. If they acknowledged Jesus' resurrection, that would mean they would have to give up their biases.

Jesus' eminent resurrection was such a reality even to those who hated Him that some of the Pharisees even paid money to spread a lie that Jesus was not raised out of the dead.[60] Why did these wayward leaders go through such great lengths to deny His resurrection? I believe deep in their thoughts they knew of the surety of Jesus' resurrection.

Even though they bore false witness concerning Jesus rebuilding the natural temple in three days, they actually knew the truth that Jesus would indeed be raised out of death on the third day.[61] This is one of the reasons they begged for guards to watch His tomb and spread the lie that Jesus' body was stolen. First, the Pharisees knew the Scriptures, and they were told that the resurrection of Jesus happened.

*Matthew 28:9-15: [9]And as they went to tell his disciples, behold, **Jesus met them,** saying, All hail. And they came and held him by the feet, and worshipped him.[10]Then said Jesus unto them, be not afraid: go tell my brethren that they **go into Galilee, and there shall they see me.** [11]Now when they were going, behold, **some of the watch came into the city, and shewed unto the chief priests all the things that were done.** [12]And when they were assembled with the elders, and had taken counsel, **they gave large money unto the soldiers,** [13]Saying, say ye, His disciples came by night, and stole him away while we slept. [14]And if this come to the governor's ears, we will persuade him, and secure you. [15]So they took the money and did as they were taught: and this saying is commonly reported among the Jews **until this day.***

The Pharisees paid the Roman soldiers (representatives of the beast system of that day) to say that Jesus was not resurrected. The Pharisees bribed the soldiers after their first attempt failed to prevent the resurrection of Jesus.

They foolishly attempted to prevent Jesus' resurrection by sealing the tomb and setting a watch at the tomb's stone. That didn't work, as we know! Next, for the Roman soldiers, they used a bribe **again** to make a false witness against Jesus' resurrection. The first bribe was given to Judas.

The same is true for some today, in principle. When some waste their money on the beast system of today (the world systems), rather than give towards the work of Jesus, they are indirectly testifying against the resurrection of Jesus. Overspending on the world is like giving money to Judas and the Roman soldiers.

They are saying that Christ is not raised; **because the Scriptures teach that tithe to Jesus (our living Melchizedek) testifies of Jesus' resurrection.**[62] In addition, there were **more than** five hundred witnesses that supersede the false witness of the bribe of the Pharisees.

Seen by More Than Five Hundred Witnesses

*1 Corinthians 15:5-8: [5]And that he was **seen of Cephas,** then **of the twelve:** [6]After that, he was seen of **above five hundred brethren** at once; of whom the greater part remains unto this present, but some are fallen asleep. [7]After that, he was **seen of James,** then of **all the apostles.** [8]And last of all he was **seen of me (Paul) also**, as of one born out of due time.*

In the days of Jesus there were many witnesses of His resurrection. There were more than five hundred men who **saw** the resurrected Jesus. When we include the ladies (who were among the first to see the resurrected Jesus), more witnesses are to be added.

The Lord God also went as far as to raise other saints from the dead soon <u>after</u> Jesus' resurrection. These saints whom God raised from the dead were also resurrected, living witnesses.

Page | 23

The eleven apostles were also witnesses of Jesus' resurrection, even though they were a little afraid of Jesus when they saw Jesus after His resurrection.

The Scripture was very transparent as to the "affect" of Jesus' resurrection when He appeared to the "eleven." The Scripture stated that the disciples became afraid, and thought they saw a spirit[63] when they saw the resurrected Jesus. This shows that the disciples also did not fully believe in His resurrection until Jesus appeared to them to show them that He is indeed raised from the dead.

Our God is so transparent, He let this fact be written. If God was insecure concerning the reality of resurrection, He could have hidden the disciples' fear and disbelief. However, the fact of resurrection does not have to be proven, it is understood as reality. Jesus' Resurrection is a truth of our inheritance that we will be resurrected also!

*Luke 24:36-40: [36]And as they thus spoke, **Jesus himself stood in the middle of them,** and says unto them, Peace be unto you. [37]But they were **terrified and affrighted and** supposed that they had seen a **spirit.** [38]And he said unto them, why are you troubled? And why do thoughts arise in your hearts? [39]Behold my hands and my feet, that it is I myself: handle me, and see; for a spirit hath not flesh and bones, as you see me have. [40] And when he had thus spoken, he shewed them his hands and his feet.*

If Jesus was not resurrected, then why would God be so transparent with respect to the "fear" the disciples expressed when they saw that a person (Jesus) can indeed be resurrected. Their surprise tells us that they did not really believe either until Jesus appeared to them. Their surprise also tells us that Jesus was indeed raised from the dead, according to the Scriptures. If it did not happen, why were they afraid?

Thus, as Paul indicated, Jesus "was **seen of Cephas,** then **of the twelve."** According to Paul, Jesus was also seen by more than "five hundred **brethren 'at once;'"** and Paul was familiar with some of them who were still alive in those days along with Paul. What a great testimony of the resurrection of Jesus. His resurrection <u>was not kept a secret</u>. Jesus wanted the whole earth to know that He restored endless life to humanity.

Jesus then appeared to James, whom I believe to be James His brother. Jesus' appearance to James is significant relative to James' apparent contradictory teaching[64] to Paul's. Paul taught that justification is by faith and not of works.

James taught that we are "justified by works" and that "faith is made perfect" by "works." And by the way, there is no contradiction; one should understand the revelation of the two teachings. Paul who **labored** more that all of them is right; and James, the Lord's brother, is also right.

Jesus then appeared to Paul on more than one occasion. Paul was the last of the early apostles to see the resurrected Jesus, "And last of all he was **seen of me (Paul) also**...." Paul was so convinced of the resurrection of Jesus that he jeopardized his life for Jesus. Why?

He knew that Jesus was able to raise him up again if he died. Paul was so convinced of Jesus' resurrection that he labored more than all the other apostles. He fully occupied himself with the suffering of Jesus if by any means, through suffering even until death, he may experience the resurrection out of the dead.[65]

The living "flesh and bone"[66] Jesus appeared unto "many" to witness to them of His resurrection; and He also appeared for them to testify the same to the nations, even in dangerous situations. Why were they so bold about our Lord Jesus Christ?

They were convinced He could raise them from the dead if they were inadvertently killed like Paul, who was at one point "legally" dead, and whom the Lord raised again from the dead. Yes! Paul, himself, experienced being raised from the dead after being stoned by the Jews. And if you know anything about Jews stoning a person, it was to the death.[67]

*Acts 14:19-20: [19]And there came thither certain Jews from Antioch and Iconium, who persuaded the people, and, having stoned Paul, drew him out of the city, **supposing** he had been dead.[20]Howbeit, as the disciples stood round about him, he **rose up**, and came into the city: and the next day he departed with Barnabas to Derbe.*

A casual glance at verses above may imply that they **"supposed"** that Paul was dead. However, the Greek word translated as **"supposing"** literally denotes **"to do by law."** Thus, by the Jewish "law" of stoning a person, Paul's stoning was unto death.[68]

However, after the saints surrounded Paul and prayed for him, Paul **"rose up"** from the dead. There is resurrection life through Jesus in this life, and there are many witnesses of His resurrection. Paul also experienced it!

God wanted all the generations and the ages to come to know that Jesus was indeed raised from the dead. God declared His record of Jesus' life through the many witnesses. He wanted us (we who apply His blood to our hearts through faith in Jesus,) to know that we can also live in Him and with Him. This was exemplified again when God also **"emphasized"** Jesus' resurrection during that time with another resurrection.

Matthew 27:50-53: [50]Jesus, when he had cried again with a loud voice, yielded up the ghost. [51]And, behold, the veil of the temple was rent in twain from the top to the bottom; and the earth did quake, and the rocks rent; ⁵²*And the graves were opened;* **and many bodies of the saints which slept arose,** ⁵³*And came out of the graves* **after** *his resurrection, and went into the holy city, and* **appeared (or, emphasized)** *unto many.*

Our God, the living God is so awesome. His "untraceable" wisdom is to be praised. God did indeed raise Jesus from the dead. However, He did not stop there.

He raised other saints from the dead. These resurrected saints went about "the holy city" (Jerusalem). They went about the holy city to **"emphasize"** Jesus' resurrection and their own resurrection, which occurred <u>after</u> Jesus' resurrection.

The Greek word translated as "appeared" Matthew 27:53 is **"emphanizo."** One can clearly see the association or transliteration of our English word "emphasis," and "emphasize" from this Greek word.

This word and its associated root are translated in the King James Version as appear, **declare, inform,** manifest, shew (show), **openly,** and signify." It also means to **exhibit.** Thus, some of the saints who were sleeping (or dead) prior to Jesus' resurrection were raised from the dead **<u>after</u>** Jesus as **"exhibits."**

These resurrected saints went into the holy city to **emphasize** the resurrection of Jesus. They **"openly declared"** His resurrection! They **"informed"** the holy city of Jesus' resurrection! If you will, they **"emphasized"** Jesus' resurrection.

These "saints" were **"exhibits"** of the reality of resurrection; and God made sure that He **"openly"** had plenty of witnesses that the resurrection of Jesus is indeed true. Who are these "saints" who were raised, after Jesus, to testify of His resurrection? I believe these are the saints who believed Jesus would be raised from the dead in three days when Jesus preached to the dead.[69]

Abraham, Isaac, Jacob, Joseph' Bones

*Hebrews 11:22: By faith Joseph, when he died, made mention of the departing of the children of Israel; and gave commandment concerning his **bones.***

*Genesis 50:25: And Joseph took an oath of the children of Israel, saying, God will surely visit you, and you shall **carry up my bones from hence.***

*Joshua 24:32: And the **bones of Joseph,** which the children of Israel brought up out of Egypt, buried they in **Shechem,** in a parcel of ground which Jacob bought of the sons of Hamor the father of Shechem for a hundred pieces of silver: and it became the inheritance of the children of Joseph.*

*Acts 7:15-16: [15]So Jacob went down into Egypt, and died, **he, and our fathers,** [16]And were carried over into **Sychem,** and laid in the sepulcher that Abraham bought for a sum of money of the sons of Emmor the father of Sychem.*

*Genesis 50:5: **My father (Jacob)** made me swear, saying, Lo, I die: in my grave which I have dug for me in the land of Canaan, there shall you bury me ....*

Abraham and Isaac were buried in Sychem—in the land of Canaan. Jacob, Joseph (for sure), and perhaps the rest of Joseph's brothers had their bones and/or bodies carried from Egypt to the land of Canaan. Canaan is the Promised Land that eventually became Israel. This is important to know to understand who are among the "Saints" that were resurrected **after** Jesus' resurrection.

Jesus was raised from the dead in the land of Israel, the same place where Abraham, Isaac, Jacob,[70] the bones of Joseph and the body of the other patriarchs were buried. They knew that one day there would be a resurrection of the Messiah, and thus went through great lengths to have their bones and bodies placed in the Promised Land.

They walked with God "by faith;" thus they must have "heard"[71] God "say" there would be a resurrection of Jesus; and that they too would be raised from the dead <u>after</u> Jesus. Consequently, these patriarchs are among the **"many bodies of the saints which...arose... and came out of the graves <u>after</u> Jesus' resurrection."** I also believe (I repeat this is my Scriptural "opinion") that John, the Baptist, was also among the "bodies of the **saints"** that were raised from the dead.

John, the Baptist Resurrected

*Matthew 27:50-53: [50]Jesus, when he had cried again with a loud voice, yielded up the ghost. [51]And, behold, the veil of the temple was rent in twain from the top to the bottom; and the earth did quake, and the rocks rent; [52]And the graves were opened; **and many bodies of the saints which slept arose,** [53]And came out of the graves **after his resurrection,** and went into the holy city, and **appeared (or, emphasized)** unto many.*

Matthew 27:52, made it clear that "many bodies of the **saints** which slept arose." The phrase can also be translated as "the bodies of the **holy-ones" (Greek hagios) arose.** John, the Baptist was considered an **"holy one" (hagios),** as noted in Mark 6:20. So, it seems plausible to me that John, the Baptist was among those who were part of the second phase of Jesus' pattern of resurrection.

> *For Herod feared **John,** knowing that he was a just man and a **holy (hagios),** and observed him; and when he heard him, he did many things, and heard him gladly (Mark 6:20).*

Was John holy? Yes! Jesus declared that there was none greater that John born from women.[72] Heron perceived John to be a "holy-one. It is also worthy to note, as John's predecessor, Elijah was spared from experiencing sleep in death for thousands of years; Elijah being taken **alive** directly to heaven; so likewise, I believe John who was executed for speaking the truth, was raised from sleep not too long after he died. He was raised from sleep with the saints ("holy-ones") who were resurrected **after** Jesus.

As Elijah did not experience thousands of years un-resurrected (Elijah was translated to heaven), John did not experience staying in the grave for thousands of years. Just like Elijah, John, the Baptist, was spared the long duration (2,000 years and counting) of waiting until the first resurrection.

The Scripture specifically calls the dead body of John a **"corpse" (Greek: ptoma)** which means **something fallen, a fall, to plunge, collapse, ruin defeat, downfall, and so on.** "Ptoma" is also used of the "body" of the two witnesses in Revelation 11 who were raised from the dead after three and a half days. Thus, the use of the word "ptoma" (fall or corpse) relates to a fall with the view of that fallen entity standing up again (resurrected) few days after the "fall."

Matthew 24:28, NKJ: For wherever the **carcass (Gk.: ptoma)**[73] *is, there the eagles will be gathered together.*

Mark 6:29: And when his [John, the Baptist's] disciples heard of it, they came and took up his **corpse [Gk.: ptoma(Greek texts)]** *and laid it in a tomb.*

Mark 15:43-45: [43]*Joseph of Arimathea, an honorable counsellor, which also waited for the kingdom of God, came, and went in boldly unto Pilate, and craved the* **body of Jesus**. [44]*And Pilate marveled if he were already dead: and calling unto him the centurion, he asked* *him whether he had been any while dead. ⁴⁵And when he knew it of the centurion, he gave the* **body [ptoma (per the Alexandrian texts)]** *to Joseph.*

Revelation 11:8; 11: ⁸And their **dead bodies (Gk.: ptoma)** *[shall lie] in the street of the great city, which spiritually is called Sodom and Egypt, where also our Lord was crucified … ¹¹**And after three days and a half the Spirit of life from God entered into them, and they stood upon their feet;** and great fear fell upon them which saw them.*

"Ptoma" is also used in Revelation 11:8 for the "fallen body" of the two witnesses. These two witnesses' **"dead bodies" (lit., fall (singular))** were raised from the dead after three and a half days by the Spirit of Life out of God. Thus, the use of the word "ptoma" (fall or corpse) relates to a fall with the view of that fallen entity standing up again **few** days after the "fall."

This principle is also true for Jesus. Jesus stood up again, in resurrection, when His apparent "carcass" ("ptoma") was resurrected after three days and three nights. It follows that the two witnesses also stood up again after their fall ("ptoma"), after 3 ½ days. With that said, John, the Baptist also came in the "power of Elijah" (which includes resurrection power).

John did not do any miracle (sign) that may relate to "power."[74] And since the Scripture cannot be broken, and the Scripture stated that John came in "the spirit and **power** of Elijah," somehow "power" had to be fulfilled in John's life.[75] The Scripture is clear that John's power[76] is related to turning the hearts of fathers to children and the hearts of children to fathers. Yet, the power of the Holy Spirit in John's life **also** relates to not being subjected to death, similarly to Elijah. Thus, John was not subjected to death for too long; and he was resurrection from the dead just after Jesus was resurrected.[77]

*Revelation 11:7-11: ⁷And when they shall have finished their testimony, the beast that ascends out of the bottomless pit shall make war against them, and shall overcome them, and **kill** them. ⁸ And their **dead bodies** (lit., ptoma (fall)) shall lie in the street …. ¹¹And after three days and a half the **Spirit of life from God entered** into them, and they **stood upon** their feet; and great fear fell upon them which saw them.*

The resurrection of the two witnesses, cited above, who had fallen ("ptoma") is consistent with the use of this same word ("ptoma") concerning Jesus and John, the Baptist. The dead bodies of Jesus and John, the Baptist were also called "a fall;" because they were **soon** to be raised from the dead.

Jesus' "fallen 'carcass'" stood up again (He was resurrected from the dead) after three days by the power of God. The two witnesses in Revelation stood up after three and a half days by the Spirit of Life from God. It is my opinion (Scripturally based) that John's time in death, was relatively short.

Remember as I indicated earlier, John **also** came in the **"power of Elijah."**[78] Thus, the Scripture had to be fulfilled in John's relative to the power of life. The prophets prophesied until John, but from John's days until now, the Scriptures are being fulfilled.[79] John fulfilled "the spirit and power of Elijah." For example, he turned hearts. It follows that the "spirit and power of Elijah" relative to overcoming death must also be fulfilled in John's life.

Elijah was taken to heaven never to see death. This is one of the examples of the power of Elijah with respect to God's power working in Elijah. Elijah was spared from being in "sleep" for thousands of years because God took him alive to heaven. Similarly, it appears that John's corpse was among the bodies of the saints that were resurrected shortly after Johns' death, **after** Jesus' resurrection.

Like Jesus and Elijah, I believe John was spared longevity in sleep (death). Was John a "saint?" Yes! Was he "asleep" before Jesus' resurrection? Yes! Was his death defined as a "fall?" Yes! His death is a "fall" that relates to imminent resurrection. Was he among the saints that were raised from the dead after Jesus' resurrection? What disqualified him from being raised after Jesus? Nothing!

The Lord said, John, the Baptist was the greatest prophet who ever lived. And Jesus, also called John, the Baptist, the greatest prophet. **If you noticed in the Scripture, Jesus did not make any comments when He was told of John's death.**[80] Why did Jesus not make any response concerning John's death? Jesus knew that there would be a resurrection of many of the saints soon after His resurrection. John is among the saints!

Thus, in conclusion, the saints highlighted in this section exemplified the resurrected saints (after Jesus' resurrection) who, in turn, **emphasized** the resurrection of Jesus. Remember "Abraham rejoiced to see [Jesus'] day."[81] Therefore, it must have been a "joy" for Abraham to **"exhibit"** how his Lord (Jesus, the Christ) resurrected his body. It must have been especially joyous for Abraham knowing that Jesus preached His resurrection to both the dead in Abraham's Bosom, and the dead in Hades, which were only separated by a gulf between those on the side of the comforted and those on the side of the tormented.[82]

Maybe Joseph emphasized in the holy city, "Jesus has indeed allowed me to partake of the true "exodus." He raised (exodus) **"my bones** out of the dead!" Can you hear Isaac, the man of meditation, saying, "The **greater Promised Seed** has indeed kept His promise to His seed and caused me (one of His seed) to **laugh** in resurrected life!" Jacob (he whose thigh the angel broke) may have said, "I 'Jeshurun'[83] have indeed been 'straightened out' in resurrection!" I believe these are some of the saints that were raised from the dead and who believed the preaching of Jesus while Jesus was in the heart of the earth for three days and three nights.

Jesus also preached His Resurrection to them that are dead

1 Peter 4:6: For, for this cause was the gospel preached also to them that are dead, that they might be judged according to men in the flesh, but live according to God in the spirit.

The question must be asked, what was Jesus preaching? The answer is He preached His resurrection! He preached the same thing to the dead as He declared to the living. Jesus' message does not change like some today. I believe Jesus also said to the dead in Hades (both compartments), "For **as Jonas** was **three days** and **three nights** in the whale's belly; so, shall the **Son of man** be **three days** and **three nights.**

Jesus preached the same message to the dead, while He was in Death and Hades before He was raised from the dead! Could you imagine the thoughts of those who had been dead or sleep for millenniums? They had seen lots of people join them in death through the ages,[84] but they had never seen any rise again, permanently. They were among the **imprisoned spirits.**[85]

Subsequently, there must have been among them unbelief concerning resurrection, just as it is in the land of the living. However, for those in the heart of the earth who believed Jesus' words, they were raised from the dead.[86] This resurrection of the saints occurred **after** Jesus' resurrection. "For this cause was the **gospel preached** also to them that are **dead,** that they might be judged according to men in the flesh, but live according to God in the spirit" **(1Peter 4:6).**

They were raised **after** Jesus; because Jesus is "the firstborn from the dead; that **in all things** he might have the

preeminence."[87] Yes, "it was impossible for death to keep its hold on [Jesus];" and the same was true of saints who God destined to be raised after Jesus.[88] The same is true for us who now belong to Christ, Jesus. We will be raised from the dead "'in' the resurrection of the 'righteous.'"

Therefore, "We having the **same spirit of faith,** according as it is written, I believed, and therefore have I spoken; we also believe, and therefore speak; **knowing** that he which raised up the Lord Jesus shall raise up us also by Jesus and shall present us with you."[89]

Prayer opportunity:

If you are not sure if you will partake of the better resurrection, here is a prayer you can pray to Jesus. "Lord Jesus, I confess with my mouth that the Lord Jesus is the Christ; and I believe in my heart that Jesus died for my sins and that God has raised Jesus from the dead for my justification. Because, in my heart I believe that Jesus is the Christ unto righteousness and with my mouth confession is made unto salvation." Amen! *(See 1 John 5:1 w/Rom 10:9-10)*

Date and Time of Prayer: _____

Resurrection of the Firstfruit Christ

1 Corinthians 15:20-23: *[20]But now is Christ risen from the dead and become the **firstfruits of them that slept**. [21]For since by man came death, by man also came the resurrection of the dead. [22]For as in Adam all die, even so in Christ shall all be made alive. [23]But every man in his own order: **Christ the firstfruits**; afterward, they that are Christ's at his coming.*

I will begin this chapter by first defining **"firstfruits Christ."**[90] "Firstfruits" is singular in the Greek in all the New Testament verses the word is used. Therefore, it should be written as firstfruit (singular). In relation to resurrection, the "firstfruit Christ" will be **the first <u>corporate group</u>** of believers who become just like Jesus Christ,[91] including being raised from the dead after a short stay in a fallen state. In the past, some like Paul, Peter, John, and disciples at Antioch became so much like Jesus, they were called Christians.[92]

However, some of Jesus' mature believers, as "one new man," will also fulfill the pattern of Jesus, the firstfruit, with regards to resurrection. It is also worthy to note that there is a difference between a firstfruit believer and firstfruit Christ. This "firstfruit" believer includes believers who were/are the first to follow Jesus from their respective nations.[93] Whereas, the "firstfruit Christ" will be resurrected not too long after their death.[94]

This resurrection of the corporate firstfruit Christ is considered "part" of the first resurrection. The Bible shows the "firstfruit Christ" as those who will be raised from the dead soon after they are killed for preaching "the prophecy" — the testimony of Jesus. After the beast eventually kills them, they will not have to wait thousands of years to be raised from the dead like the other disciples or saints throughout the past ages.

The corporate firstfruit Christ will be like Jesus in their resurrection; except **Jesus has the preeminence in all things.**[95] Like Jesus, they will be raised from the dead few days after their apparent "fall." Jesus was raised from the dead in three (3) days; the firstfruit Christ will be raised after three and a half (3 ½) days. This firstfruit, who will be resurrected through the Spirit of Life, is considered as the "first" in rank of the first resurrection. That is, the firstfruit resurrection is the first "course" of the first resurrection, with the second phase of the first resurrection occurring when Jesus comes, physically, in the seventh or last trumpet.

Now that I have defined the firstfruit Christ, let us discuss the **"resurrection"** of the firstfruit Christ. As stated before, it appears that the resurrection of firstfruit Christ is also synonymous with the first resurrection; that is, it is one of the courses of the first resurrection. Paul indicated that there will be four resurrections in 1 Corinthians 15:20-26.

In 1 Corinthians 15, there is the resurrection of Jesus "Christ ... **the firstfruit** of those who have fallen asleep." Then, there is the resurrection of the "firstfruit Christ;" after this, the resurrection of "those who are Christ's at His coming." Finally, there is the resurrection at "the end," at which resurrection the last enemy (Death) is destroyed.

This "end" resurrection is also called "the resurrection ... of eternal judgment." Like Paul in 1 Corinthians 15, John in the book of Revelation 20 also discusses the first resurrection and the resurrection of the rest of the dead after the millennium. This is the resurrection related to "the conclusion" or "the goal" where the last enemy, Death, and Hell, will be destroyed.

With that said, the first resurrection, <u>which has phases,</u> also includes the resurrection of the "firstfruit Christ." There are orders or ranks in "the first resurrection."

*Revelation 20:6, NKJ: Blessed and holy is he who has **part (or lit., course)** in the first resurrection. Over such the second death has no power, but they shall be priests of God and of Christ and shall reign with Him a thousand years.*

*1 Corinthians 15:22-24, NKJ: 22For as in Adam all die, even so in Christ all shall be made alive. 23But each one in his own **order (or rank):** Christ the firstfruits, afterward those who are Christ's at His coming. 24Then comes the end when He delivers the kingdom to God the Father....*

The truth of these "ranks" and "courses" was not known to all in some of the recent ages because the Greek text was not readily available for many years. Proper translation of the Greek texts is important to fully appreciate the different "courses" (phases) and ranks of the first resurrection.

The phrase **"Christ the firstfruit"** in **1 Corinthians 15:23** was also not translated correctly in most versions. The proper translation of 1 Corinthians 15:23 highlight the ranks or phases in the resurrections. Thus, it is so wonderful that we now have access to the Greek versions. It is also important to know that Young's Literal Translation and others did translate 1 Corinthians 15:23 correctly from the Greek text as we will see in a moment. With that said, for clarity, this is the order of the resurrections, again.

First, Jesus, who is both Lord and Christ, is **"the** firstfruit of them that slept."[96] We discussed this already. "Christ the firstfruit" is different from "firstfruit Christ." There will then be the resurrection of "the firstfruit Christ." This resurrection is also a phase of the first resurrection as cited by John in

Revelation 20:4-6. Again, as indicated earlier, the first resurrection has **"courses"** or **phases** just as Jesus' pattern resurrection had two phases.

Jesus was raised from the dead (this is the first phase) and "thereupon" the bodies of the saints who slept were raised soon "after His resurrection" (this is the second phase of Jesus' pattern resurrection). Thus, after Jesus was raised from the dead, there were other "bodies" of saints that were also resurrected.

In the "'**first**' resurrection," as named in Revelation 20:4-6, there are also two (2) courses. There is the first phase of the first resurrection consisting of the firstfruit Christ, which is the resurrection of the "two witnesses." The "two witnesses"[97] are also known as the "two olive trees,"[98] "the two sons of oil,"[99] "the two candlesticks,"[100] and "the two prophets"[101] as outlined in Revelation11:1-11.

Remember, these are they that will remain dead only for a short time similarly to Jesus; except, Jesus has the preeminence in all things. Jesus has the preeminence because God raised Jesus from the dead after three (3) days. However, it will take a little longer, three and a half (3 ½) days, for God to raise the two witnesses.

Then, there is the second phase of the first resurrection. These are those who will be raised in the coming of Jesus according to 1 Thessalonians 4:13-18 and Revelation 20:4-6. Paul said in 1 Thessalonians 4:16, "The dead in Christ shall **rise first.**" Since, the dead in Christ shall rise **first,** they must be part of the **first** resurrection in Revelation 20: 1-6. In Revelation 20:5, John said "Blessed and holy is he who part in the **first resurrection** ...." With that said, to really appreciate the concept of the resurrection of the firstfruit Christ, I must now show the difference between translating the Scriptures as "Christ, the firstfruit" and "firstfruit Christ."

Firstfruit Christ in lieu of Christ the Firstfruit

"Firstfruit Christ" in lieu of "Christ the firstfruit" is an important concept to understand, which clarifies the original meaning **intended** by the apostle Paul. This understanding that "Christ, the firstfruit" in 1 Corinthians 15:23 is literally "firstfruit Christ" will clarify the incorrect meaning the English translators inadvertently conveyed by translating the Greek text as "Christ, the firstfruits."

This phrase "firstfruit Christ" was not fully known by the general assembly of the Church, because most translations or translators did not make available the Greek texts used for verifying translations.[102] There was a time when the Bibles were kept chained to podiums and were translated only in Latin to be read by the priests. The uneducated populous could not understand or properly read the Bible.

Remember also that translations of the Greek or Latin texts into common vernacular were not available to the general populous until after John Wycliffe, Martin Luther, and after the printing press was invented in the 1500s. After a while, interlinear Bibles (Bibles having the same text in various languages set in alternate lines) were made available with the Greek texts. With that said, the Greek texts for 1 Corinthians 15:23 all read as such:

*1 Corinthians 15:23, Alexandrian Text, Nestle-Aland 27th Edition: Hékastos dé en toó idíoo tágmati **aparcheé Christós** épeita hoi toú Christoú en teé parousía autoú.*

*1 Corinthians 15:23, Received Text, Interlinear Scripture Analyzer: Hékastos dé en toó idíoo tágmati **aparcheé Christós** épeita hoi toú Christoú en teé parousía autoú.*

1 Corinthians 15:23, Majority Text, Robinson-Pierpoint: *Hékastos dé en toó idíoo tágmati* **aparcheé Christós** *épeita hoi toú Christoú en teé parousía autoú.*

1 Corinthians 15:23, Darby: *But each in his own rank:* **[the] firstfruits, Christ;** *then those that are the Christ's at his coming.*

1 Corinthians 15:23, YLT: *And each in his proper order,* **a firstfruit Christ,** *afterwards those who are the Christ's, in his presence.*

As one reads the references above one sees that the phrase translated as "Christ the firstfruit" in 1 Corinthians 15:23 was originally written as **"firstfruit Christ" ("aparcheé Christós").** This understanding is now available to all the saints who are willing to research.

And as indicated earlier, it is also available in printed interlinear Bibles. Most Bible software also has the Greek versions included. Darby's translation and Young's Literal Translation of 1 Corinthians 15:23 also show the correct rendering (a person can buy these translations in most Bible bookstores).

With that said, there is Jesus, the Christ who is indeed "**the firstfruit** of them that slept."[103] Our Lord and Savior Jesus Christ has the **preeminence** in **all** things as indicated in the Scriptures and cited prior to this chapter. Jesus is indeed **"the"** preeminent "firstfruit" of all! Jesus is the firstborn of the Church of the firstborns.

Jesus is the first of the firstfruit. However, even though Jesus is indeed "the firstfruit of them that slept," there is also "firstfruit Christ." Firstfruit Christ in its definition points to the first group of believers to reign as Christ, or the first group of believers to become just like Jesus while living on earth. It was always God's plan to also have a corporate firstfruit Christ.

These are the ones who will be the first from among **the saints** to become just like Jesus Christ. At the end of this age, there will be a corporate people who will be considered as the first to become like Jesus. Like Jesus, the firstfruit Christ will also be killed for their witness of Jesus, as Jesus was crucified for His testimony. The firstfruit Christ will also be raised from the dead soon after their death, just like Jesus is the firstfruit to be raised from the dead permanently.

Jesus was the first "man" to be raised from the dead never to experience death again after three (3) days. So likewise, there will be a **"group"** of Christ-like believers who will also be among the first group to become that "perfect man," **a "'mature' [corporate] man."**[104] Except, these "first" to become like Jesus (the first group to reign over death like Jesus) will be raised after three and a half (3 ½) days.

These two witnesses will be resurrected as "firstfruit Christ" by the "Spirit of Life from God,"[105] with the understanding that the rest of those in Christ will also be raised in turn in the coming of the Lord Jesus. With all the above now reviewed, let us look at 1 Corinthians 15:23 in "context" of its "pretext," 1 Corinthians 15:22.

Made Alive in the Christ

1 Corinthians 15:22-23: [22]*For as in Adam all die, even so **in Christ (lit., the Christ)** shall all be made alive.* [23]***But every man in his own order: 'firstfruit Christ;'*** *afterward they that are Christ's at his coming.*

Before I cite some other translations of these verses, let us look at the context of 1 Corinthians 15:23 relative to 1 Corinthians 15:22. In 1 Corinthians 15:22, the subject is **"all being made alive 'in the Christ'."** 1 Corinthians 15:23 is a continuation of 1 Corinthians 15:22 and is connected by the conjunction "but."

Thus, the people who will be made alive in 1 Corinthians 15:23 are those who will be made alive "in the Christ." 1 Corinthians 15:23 is not referring to Jesus Christ Himself being made alive. 1 Corinthians 15:23 is referring to those who belong to Jesus being made alive "in the Christ;" and these believers who are made alive "in the Christ" consist of "ranked" groups, **"firstfruit Christ"** and **"they that are Christ's** 'in' His coming."

In 1 Corinthians 15:23 the phrase "shall all be made alive" is future tense in the Greek texts. Jesus is already raised from the dead, never to die again. That is, Jesus' resurrection already occurred in the context of 1 Corinthian 15:20. In I Corinthians 15:20, the word "risen" is perfect tense in the Greek text which means that Jesus' resurrection already occurred in the past.

1 Corinthians 15:22-23, YLT: *²²for even as in Adam all die, so also in the Christ all shall be made alive,* *²³and each in his proper order, a firstfruit Christ, afterwards those who are the Christ's, in his presence.*

1 Corinthians 15:23, Darby: But each in his own rank: [the] firstfruits, Christ; then those that are the Christ's at his coming.

Young's Literal Translation" along with Darby's translation translated the Greek text correctly. 1 Corinthians 15:23 which follows 1 Corinthians 15:22, connected by the Greek conjunction "de" (but, yet) is indeed referring to two ranks of resurrections. These groups will be raised from the dead in their own rank, order, or course.

Course in the First Resurrection

---

1 Corinthians 15:22-23: *²²... in Christ (lit., in the Christ) shall all be made alive.* *²³But every man in his own order....*

*Revelation 20:6: Blessed and holy is he that hath **part (or course)** in the first resurrection....*

*1 Corinthians 14:27: If any man speak in an unknown tongue, let it be by two, or at the most by three, and that by **course**....*

In reference to all being made alive in the Christ, Paul indicated that "every man" will be raised "in his own **order.**" "Order" is defined in the Greek as **rank, ordered position, a group, class, and a set sum.** Thus, there are **"groups"** in the resurrections.

There are also **"ranks"** in the resurrection. In fact, the "seed" (the type of Word they hear) that one allows to be planted in them determines the rank of "the glory" one will receive in the resurrection. There are "different" degrees of glory, according to the Scriptures.[106] Therefore, there are also "ranks." There is also **"part,"** or **"course"** in the first resurrection.

The Greek word for **"part" used** in Revelation 20:6 is also translated as **"course"** in 1 Corinthians 14:27. In 1 Corinthians 14:27, it mentions that at the "most" three (3) persons are to speak in an unknown tongue "and that by **course."** In other words, if tongues are to be spoken in a meeting, speak by taking turns ("course").

"At the most ... **three"** should speak in **"course."** It follows that according to this usage of the Greek word "meros" (a part, course, etc.), the "part" in the first resurrection involves "course." This "course" is witnessed in 1 Corinthians 15:23, 1 Thessalonians 4:13-18, 1 Corinthians 15:51-52 and Revelation 20:4-6.

The first course or part in the first resurrection is the two witnesses as defined by John in Revelation 11. The second course or part in the first resurrection is those defined by John in Revelation 20:4 and by Paul in 1 Thessalonians 4:13-18 and 1 Corinthians 15:51-52.

In other words, the first resurrection **courses** consist of "firstfruit Christ" and "the dead in Christ who shall rise first" in their respective "order." The two witnesses are the "beginning" fruits. The other firstfruit course to follow in the first resurrection is the saints who belonged to Christ in their own "order" (rank). In the words of Paul, every person who belongs to Jesus will be raised from the dead in his/her turns and according to his or her ranks.

There is an ordered rank in the first resurrection. There will be some in whom God demonstrates His domination over death "first" by allowing the Spirit of Life from God to raise them from the dead after three and a half (3 ½) days. Then there will be the resurrection of the second phase of the first resurrection in the coming of our Lord Jesus.

The Firstfruit Reign

---

*1 Corinthians 15:23 (transliterated): Hékastos dé en toó idíoo tágmati **aparcheé Christós** ....*

1 Corinthians 15:22-23, YLT: [22]*For even as in Adam all die, so also in the Christ all shall be made alive,* [23] *and each in his proper order, a firstfruit Christ....*

The Greek word **"Aparcheé"** used in "aparcheé Christós" (firstfruit Christ) is a compound of two words: "apo" which means "from" and "archomai," the middle voice of "arho." Archo and archomai means **to commence in order of time, first, reign, rule, beginning, the beginning of a sacrifice, firstlings of a sacrifice.**

When you put the two words together, they mean: **from-first, from-reign, from-rule, from-beginning, from earliest ripe of**

the crop, from-firstlings of a sacrifice, etc. The root word for "archomai," the word "archo," is used in two places in the Bible in which it is translated as "rule over" and "reign over."

Romans 15:12: And again, Esaias says, there shall be a root of Jesse, and he that shall rise to reign over (archo) the Gentiles; in him shall the Gentiles trust.

Mark 10:42: But Jesus called them to him, and says unto them, you know that they which are accounted to rule over (archo) the Gentiles exercise lordship over them; and their great ones exercise authority upon them.

Thus, firstfruit Christ carry the idea of those who will be first **after** Jesus to **"rule over"** death, or **"reign over"** death. This definition coincides with the first resurrection out of the dead ones, the resurrection of those who will be among the first to **reign** (Greek: basileou) **with** Christ for a thousand years without dying again.[107] Death will be swallowed in victory for those who rise first as firstfruit Christ and for those who are raised first in His coming.

Just as Jesus was "the" preeminent first to rule over death, there will be a group of **"sons of the resurrection"** who will walk in a similar dominion as Jesus. As "death has no more dominion over Him (Jesus)," God will raise the firstfruit Christ from the dead by His Spirit of Life.

Through the Spirit of Life from God, which is made available to all believers through Jesus, some of the firstfruit Christ will rule over death swiftly. This means they will only be able to die or be killed when it's their time to die, not before;[108] and when the firstfruit Christ is finally killed by the beast, the Spirit of Life will cause them to reign over death by raising them from the dead in short order. They will be resurrected from the dead to "stand on their feet" through the Spirit of Life who came out of God.

These firstfruit will be "the earliest ripe of the crop." The rest of the "crop" will be raised in the other course of the first resurrection. There is always a portion of a crop to ripen first. The almond tree, among the trees, is considered a tree that is the first to bud. The Hebrew definition for the "almond" tree means "wakeful" tree.

Thus, the almond tree, which blossoms in January, is the first of the fruit trees to "awake" from the sleep of "winter." This principle is true for those who will be raised just before the sounding of the "last trumpet" which is the same as the sounding of the "seventh trumpet" of the book of Revelation. There will be an almond resurrection, the firstfruit Christ of the rest of what James 5:7 calls "the precious fruit of the earth" in "the coming of the Lord."

The rod of the almond will be the first to bud in resurrection whenever the seventh trumpet is impending to sound and during the "days"[109] of the seventh trumpet, with the understanding that the seventh trumpet is synonymous with the last trumpet.

The Seventh (the Last) Trumpet

Revelation 11:15-19: [15]***And the seventh angel sounded...*** *[18]and thy wrath is come, and the* **time of the dead,** *that they should be* **judged...**[19]*And the temple of God was opened in heaven, and there was seen in his temple* **the ark** *of his testament....*

1 Corinthians 15:51-52: [51]*Behold, I shew you a mystery; we shall not all sleep, but we shall all be changed,* [52]*... at the* **last trump**... *the dead shall be raised incorruptible, and we shall be changed.*

1 Thessalonians 4:16-17, NKJ: [16]*For the Lord Himself will descend from heaven with a shout, with the voice of an archangel, and* **with the trumpet of God.** *And the dead in Christ will rise first.* [17]*Then* *we who are alive and remain shall be caught up together with them in the clouds to meet the Lord in the air ....*

Paul indicated that in the trumpet of God the dead in Christ will rise first and those who are alive at that time will be seized together with them in the clouds to meet the Lord. This is the same trumpet that is also called last trumpet. In the last trumpet, the dead will be raised incorruptible and the living saints "shall be changed." This last trumpet is the seventh trumpet in the book of Revelation. Here is one of the many ways the truth can be conveyed that the last trumpet is the seventh trumpet. In Revelation 8, we learn that the seventh seal consists of seven angels with seven trumpets.

Thus, the seventh trumpet of the seven trumpets is the last trumpet of a series of seven. According to Paul, resurrection takes place in the last trumpet. And according to John, resurrection takes place just before and during the seventh (last) trumpet.

The two apostles agree. John, in Revelation 10 and Revelation 11, points to the **"days"** of the seventh trumpet as the "last" of all seven, while Paul referencing the **"last** trumpet" points to the **"farthest"** of time during the seventh trumpet.

During the sounding of the seventh trumpet, "chronos" ("uninterrupted time") will be interrupted by an "opportune time." **"The [opportune] time[110] of the dead"** will come "that they might be **judged (lit., separated, distinguished, "called into question")."** This "separation" of "the dead" appears to <u>also</u> relate to those who have "part" in the first resurrection.[111] In other words, it appears that there will be a distinguishing of the dead by the interruption the seventh trumpet will usher in; [112] and there will be those who will rise.

As we will see later, there is evidence in Revelation 11:15-19 from the Majority Texts and the Alexandrian Texts that the Lord comes during the seventh trumpet, which corresponds to Paul's description of events scheduled to occur in the last trumpet, the trumpet of God. **Another truth that shows that the seventh trumpet is the last trumpet is the use of the phrase** "great power" — God's resurrection power.[113]

*Acts 4:33, NKJ: And with **great power** the apostles gave witness to the resurrection of the Lord Jesus. And great grace was upon them all.*

*Revelation 11:17, NKJ saying: "We give You thanks, O Lord God Almighty, The One who is and who was and who is to come, Because You have taken Your **great power** and reigned.*

We see in the references above that **"great power"** is linked to the "resurrection of the Lord Jesus." In the seventh trumpet, God's great power is acknowledged because God used it during the seventh trumpet, the last of the seven trumpets. Therefore, the first resurrection (both phases) is revealed in the seventh trumpet in various ways.

Another one of the ways the firstfruit resurrection can be understood is by the Ark of the Covenant that was seen in the **open** temple of God during the seventh trumpet. This Ark was seen during the sounding of the seventh trumpet. And in the Ark was Aaron's almond rod that blossomed — a symbol of firstfruit resurrection!

*Revelation 11:15; 19: 15**And the seventh angel sounded**... 19**And the temple of God was opened in heaven, and there was seen in his temple the ark** of his testament...*

On September 23, 2006, I remember meditating on the meaning of the Ark being seen during the seventh trumpet as it relates to the firstfruit resurrection. In my meditation, the

Lord began to give me understanding; yet I questioned, just a little, what the Holy Spirit was teaching me at the time. Suddenly, I heard audibly voice of Jesus saying the same words that were written in the Gospels, "I thank thee, O Father, Lord of heaven and earth, that you have hid these things from the wise and prudent, and have revealed them unto babes: even so, Father; for so it seemed good in thy sight."[114]

I believe, the Lord Jesus was encouraging me to hear what the Holy Spirit was teaching me. The Lord called what the Holy Spirit was teaching me a "revelation." It was the Father revealing Jesus and His Church to me through the Ark as it relates to resurrection during the seventh or last trumpet. Here is how the Ark relates to the firstfruit Christ (the almond rod).

The Ark and the Almond Rod

Revelation 11:15; 19: **¹⁵And the seventh angel sounded...** *¹⁹And the temple of God was opened in heaven, and there was seen in his temple **the ark** of his testament....*

Hebrews 9:3-4: *³And after the second veil... the Holiest of all; ⁴Which had the golden censer, and **the Ark of the Covenant overlaid** roundabout with gold, wherein was... **Aaron's rod** that **budded**....*

In the sounding of the seventh trumpet, **"the temple of God was opened in heaven, and there was seen in his temple the ark ...."** According to Paul, "the temple of God" is the Church.[115] Thus, the Church will be opened, and the Ark will be seen in her.

The "Ark of the Covenant" is foremost a symbol of Jesus, the Christ of the "New Covenant" and/or Jesus, the Christ of "the everlasting covenant." The Ark **in** the temple points to "Christ [the Ark] **in** us [His temple], the hope of glory."[116] Aaron's almond rod "in" the Ark also points to Jesus who is the firstfruit of all to be raised from the dead; yet Aaron's almond rod also points to the firstfruit "in" Christ to be raised ("budded") from the dead during the "seventh trumpet."

It is significant that Aaron's rod was an almond rod.[117] The Hebrew definitions for **almond** are: wakeful, **sleeplessness,** watcher, hastener, alert, earliest to ripe, etc. The Scripture equates "sleep" to death.[118]

Therefore, the almond being defined as the "sleeplessness" points to "deathlessness." Hence, the almond tree is also a symbol of resurrection. The firstfruit Christ is harvested from among those who are as the "almond" — those who "watch" as Christ commanded.

They "hasten" to be the "earliest" to become like Jesus in His death and resurrection as Paul strived to do in Philippians 3:10-12. I also mentioned earlier that the almond was the "first" of the fruit trees to "bud" during the "winter" (a symbol of tribulation) seasons.[119] In Numbers 17, when Moses and Aaron's appointments as leaders (first among equals) were questioned, it was Aaron's rod that God caused to blossom as a sign that they were chosen leaders of God.

Aaron's rod was the first and the only rod to blossom among the twelve rods that were stripped and placed before God; and it **"yielded almonds."** With respect to resurrection, almonds are symbols of the "earliest" to be resurrected during the first resurrection. Remember, the Ark is in the temple of God. The temple is us. The Ark is Christ. Thus, "the Ark in the temple" is a symbol of "Christ in us;" and Christ Jesus is "the resurrection and the life." In this Ark is the budding almond rod.

The temple of God will be opened, and all that the Ark represents and all that its content represents (the gold pot, the manna, Aaron's rod that budded, the tablets of the covenant, the cherubs of glory and the mercy seat) will be seen. For example, the almond buds will manifest. That is, Christ in us will be manifested in the fullness of resurrection. Next, we must also understand that Aaron, himself, also points to the Ark being "revealed" (opened) in order that the blossoming almonds may be seen.

This truth can be seen in the **hieroglyphics of Aaron's name.** Aaron's pictographic name may be interpreted to have various meanings. Aaron's pictographic name is a symbol of Jesus' resurrection as the greater Aaron.[120] Aaron's name also points to those in Christ who will be raised again from the dead. Aaron's name also means pictorially the Ark revealed.

In other words, Aaron's high priestly duty is a narrative of what the Ark represents. Saying it another way, the Ark represents Jesus, our Greater Aaron or Jesus our Melchizedek functioning as our High Priest in the Holy of Holies. The Ark also represents those who will be reigning-priests (king-priests) of God, who will be ruling with Christ, our High Priest during the seventh (7th) millennium.

The book of Revelation states that the temple of God (us) will be opened. The Ark (Jesus) was seen in the temple. According to Hebrews 9:4, <u>in</u> the Ark (Jesus) is "**Aaron's** rod that 'yielded fruit'" (a type of resurrection).[121] With that said, let's look at Aaron's name; and before, I give the pictographic definition of Aaron's name, I must also say that there are definitions provided for Aaron's name.

Aaron's name is defined as: teacher, lofty, mountain of strength, mountaineer, enlightener (Hitchcock, Jerome, Gesenius, etc.). However, Hebrew letters and thus Hebrew words were originally made up of pictures.[122] We formally call this hieroglyphic or "pictographic scripts."

The same Hebrew letters used in the spelling of **"Aaron"** are used in the spelling for the **"Ark."** The basic Hebrew[123] for Aaron is transliterated as AHRN (אהרן).[124] The transliteration of the Hebrew word for **Ark** is ARN (ארן).[125]

The difference between the two words is that there is an "H" inserted in Aaron's name–AHRN. The pictographic idea of the Hebrew letter "H" (ה) is the picture of an **open window, or an opening, and "hey" (revealed to attract attention).** When this Hebrew letter "H" is used at the end of a Hebrew word, it makes that word feminine.

However, when this letter "H" (ה) is used in the middle of a word, it means **to reveal,** to reveal the heart, to behold, and to look. For example, the Hebrew word for "tent" as in the **"Tent of the Congregation"** is the basic Hebrew word for God "EL" (אל) with an "H" inserted in the middle of EL (אהל).

Thus, the "tent" (אהל) is a place where God's (אל) is revealed or seen. This same principal applies to the Hebrew word for Father AB (אב); and the Hebrew word for love AHB (אהב); where love is the heavenly Father revealed — "God is love."

Thus "Aaron's" name is a picture of **"the heart of the Ark revealed;"** or his name pictures **"the revealed Ark;"** or Aaron's duty as high priest **reveals** what the **Ark** represents. To make this simple, Aaron's name is a symbol of the heart of Jesus revealed, as our merciful High Priest who can understand and measure our sufferings.

With that said, we also learned, when the Ark is revealed, the budded almond rod (deathlessness) is represented inside the

Ark. **"Aaron"** who is as the "revealed Ark" has in him the sleepless (deathless) almond rod. Therefore, Aaron and his rod that budded and bear fruit is a personification of Jesus (the greater Aaron) being the firstfruit to be resurrected.

Aaron, the Ark being revealed, and his "wakeful rod" being understood, also points to the firstfruit Christ being raised from the dead. In Numbers 17, Aaron's rod had no leaves or fruit when it was placed before the Lord. After one night with the Lord, the dead almond rod blossomed and bore fruit.[126]

Some of the firstfruit Christ will be killed by the beast (they will become a stripped almond rod). However, after three and a half (3 ½) days, they will blossom in resurrection through God's Spirit of Life. The Spirit of Life from God will enter the "corpse" of the firstfruit Christ (the two witnesses) to wake them from sleep. This will take place just before the seventh trumpet.

I must say, at this juncture, that the invitation to be a part and/or to be in the rank of the resurrection of the firstfruit Christ is available to all saints who will give themselves to the Lord. The firstfruit Christ is also called the two olive trees that is made up of Jews and Gentiles who believe that Jesus is the Christ. The firstfruit Christ is the two-fold sons of golden oil who supply the oil of the Holy Spirit to His Church. The firstfruit Christ is also the twofold prophetic Churches (two candlesticks) just before the last trumpet who themselves become as trumpets (prophets).

They will be called to prophesy as Jesus preached the kingdom of God in/with power. These are those who are ready to lay down their souls for Jesus. These are those who have been empowered by the outpouring of the Holy Spirit to witness prophetically and to be a part of the resurrection of the firstfruit Christ.

We just have to **"press"** into that "upward calling (or invitation) of God" like Paul exhorted in Philippians 3. It will take us knowing "Him" (Jesus) personally, and knowing **"the fellowship of His suffering,** being made conformable to His death," just like the Lord's two witnesses were made conformable to Christ's death in Revelation 11. They suffered to the point of death and were resurrected into eternal life.

Philippians 3:10; 14: [10]*That I may* **know him,** *and the* **power of his resurrection,** *and the fellowship of his sufferings,* **being made conformable unto his death;** [11]*If* **by any means** *I might attain unto the resurrection of the dead* ... [14]**I press** *toward the mark for the prize of* **the high calling** *of God in Christ Jesus.*

The First Resurrection

Revelation 20:4-6: *⁴And I saw thrones, and they sat upon them, and judgment was given unto them: and I saw the souls of them that were beheaded for the witness of Jesus, and for the word of God, and which had not worshipped the beast, neither his image, neither had received his mark upon their foreheads, or in their hands; and they lived and reigned with Christ a thousand years. ⁵But the rest of the dead lived not again until the thousand years were finished.* **This is the first resurrection.** *⁶Blessed and holy is he that hath part in the first resurrection: on such the second death hath no power, but they shall be priests of God and of Christ and shall reign with him a thousand years.*

1 Thessalonians 4:13-18, NKJ: *¹³But I do not want you to be ignorant, brethren, concerning those who have fallen asleep, lest you sorrow as others who have no hope. ¹⁴For if we believe that Jesus died and rose again, even so God will bring with Him those who sleep in Jesus. ¹⁵For this we say to you by the word of the Lord, that we who are alive and remain until* **the coming of the Lord** *will by no means precede those who are asleep. ¹⁶For the Lord Himself will descend from heaven with a shout, with the voice of an archangel, and with the trumpet of God.* **And the dead in Christ will rise first.** *¹⁷Then we who are alive and remain shall be caught up together with them in the clouds to meet the Lord in the air. And thus, we shall always be with the Lord. ¹⁸Therefore comfort one another with these words.*

1 Corinthians 15:22-23, YLT: *²²for even as in Adam all die, so also in the Christ all shall be made alive, ²³and each in his proper order,* **a firstfruit Christ,** *afterwards those who are the Christ's, in his presence.*

The first resurrection consists of the resurrection of the firstfruit Christ, the resurrection of the dead in Christ who will be raised in Jesus' coming, and the transforming of the bodies of the saints who will be alive at the coming of our Lord Jesus.

These will rule with Christ during the millennium being selected through Jesus.

When Jesus was raised as firstfruit out of the dead, God was selective. Thus, **not all** the dead were raised as firstfruit, but Jesus was raised "out of" the dead and then those bodies of the saints that followed His resurrection. So likewise, the first resurrection will consist of the firstfruit Christ and the rest of the dead in Christ in His coming. As we learned in the introduction, Jesus' pattern resurrection also consisted of two phases. So likewise, the first resurrection appears to consist of two phases. The first phase is the resurrection of **"firstborns"**[127] of the firstfruit Christ's.

The second phase of the first resurrection consists of the resurrection of the "dead in Christ" who "will rise first" at the seventh trumpet; the "they" who were seated on thrones, and "souls of them that were beheaded for the witness of Jesus, and for the word of God, and which had not worshipped the beast, neither his image, neither had received his mark upon their foreheads." With that said, let us look at the phases of the first resurrection; and if I seem to be repeating myself, I am repeating myself purposefully from different vantage points to make the understanding of the first resurrection as clear as I can.

First to Reign with Christ

We learned earlier that the Greek word **"aparcheé"** used in "aparcheé Christós" (firstfruit Christ) is a compound of two words: "apo" which means "from" and "archomai," the middle voice of "arho." "Archo" or "archomai" means **to commence in order of time, first, reign, rule, to make a beginning.**

We also learned earlier that when the two words ("apo" and "archo") are put together they mean: **from-first, from-reign, from-rule, to make a beginning-from, from-earliest ripe of the crop, etc.** The word "archo" is used in two other places in the Bible in which it is translated as "rule over" and "reign over." In Romans 15:12 it is used of Jesus "that shall rise **to reign over** the Gentiles." In Mark 10:42 it is also used of those who **"rule over** the Gentiles."

Thus, firstfruit can mean those who are from the first to rule, those who make a beginning in reigning, and so on. The Greek word for "first" in the phrase "first" resurrection means "before most," "beginning," "chief," and so on. It is a" beginning" resurrection. Thus, the first resurrection consists of those resurrected "before most."

The ones who are to be raised **after** the "before most" of the first resurrection are those at the resurrection of eternal judgment. The first resurrection marks "a beginning" of those who will "rule" with Christ. This first resurrection starts from the two witnesses, the first corporate Christ "from" those who "rule" in life like Jesus. They will be the first corporate group to be raised from the dead after a short death (3 ½ days).

The second phase of this first resurrection will be those who are raised in the coming of our Lord during the seventh or last trumpet. This phase of the first resurrection is just before the millennium rule as outlined in Revelation 19:11-20:6; and in Revelation 11:1-19.

One of the differences between the second course of the first resurrection and the first course of the first resurrection is that those who are raised in the second phase will mostly consist of all who were in the grave for a long duration. It seems to me that the first course of the first resurrection consists of the two witnesses, who did not stay dead for more than three and a half (3 ½) days.

Thus, since firstfruit literally means "from beginning" and "from-reigning" it agrees with the course (part) of the first resurrection. The first resurrection is for those who will be the "first" to be raised permanently out of the dead **to rule** with Christ. Jesus has ruled, is ruling and shall rule until God becomes "all in all."[128] Another way of saying it is: the first resurrection consist of those who are the first to conform to Jesus' image; and therefore, they will be the first group of that age to be raised out of the dead to reign <u>with</u> Christ. The second course of the first resurrection are those who are considered "in Christ" or those who belong to Christ in His coming. These will also reign with Christ in the millennium. With that said, let us now look at the people who will partake in the first resurrection.

I Saw Thrones

Revelation 20:4-6: *⁴And **I saw thrones,** and they sat upon them, and judgment was given unto them: ... and they lived and **reigned** with Christ a thousand years ... ⁶Blessed and holy is he that hath **part** in the first resurrection.*

John saw some **"thrones"** and **those who were sitting on the thrones**. These same "they" were also **"part"** of the first resurrection. Remember, the first resurrection has "parts" or "courses" which is the same word used in 1 Corinthians 14:27. In Corinthians, Paul indicated that the **"course"** can have **two** or **three** turns.

In Revelation 20:4, we see the "part" or "course" in the first resurrection includes three groups. The first group is those who were sitting upon thrones, judging; "I saw thrones, and they sat upon them, and **judgment** was given unto them."

The "they" that "sat upon" thrones are obviously ruling. If a king or a queen is on the throne the king/queen is reigning. Thus, the descriptions of these "first" in the list of believers who partake of the first resurrection are those who are judging on thrones. I believe these can represent the firstfruit Christ, who have thrones as outlined in Daniel 7:9, with the understanding that firstfruit literally means "from-reigning."

Those who were eventually sat on the thrones described by John may be those of the firstfruit who will reign in this life like Christ. They will have power over the creation like Jesus. They will testify of evil in the world, like Jesus did. They will be killed for their testimony, like Jesus was.[129]

Like Jesus, they will be hated even in their short lives. Also, after their short time in death, they will rise again like Jesus as "part" of the first resurrection and will reign with Christ in that age. The "they" that were seated on thrones may also represent all the saints that will be **seated** to judge the world and angels.

*1 Corinthians 6:1-4, YLT: ¹Dare any one of you, having a matter with the other, go to be judged before the unrighteous, and not before the saints? ²have you not known that the saints shall **judge the world**? And if by you the world is judged, are you unworthy of the smaller judgments? ³**have you not known that we shall judge messengers?** Why not then the things of life? ⁴of the things of life, indeed, then, if you may have judgment, those despised in the assembly -- these cause you to **sit**.*

Paul indicated that being "seated" is equated with administering the criterion for judgment. The saints of Corinthians were called into question for letting the unsaved "sit" in judgment concerning the things of the saints. In the discourse, Paul stated that the saints will judge the world and angels; so, he asked why they let the unsaved "sit" to judge instead of them. Therefore, in Revelation 20:1, the first to be mentioned in the resurrection are those who were "seated to judge." It appears to me that these are the saints who are seated on thrones to judge as beautifully explained by Paul. There will be a time when the saints will be raised in the first resurrection to "sit" on thrones of judgment, judging the world and angels, especially, the dragon and his angels.

With that said, the other partakers of the first resurrection are the souls that were beheaded for the testimony of Jesus ("the spirit of the prophecy") and the Word of God.

The Resurrection of Beheaded Souls

Revelation 20:4-6: [4]*... I saw the souls of them that were* **beheaded** *for the witness of Jesus, and for the word of God...and they lived and reigned with Christ a thousand years...* [6]*Blessed and holy is he that hath* **part** *in the first resurrection.*

Most read the verses above and equate being beheaded only with physical death. This is true, but not complete. "Beheaded" does point to those who will be beheaded with an ax, literally—John, the Baptist and Paul lost their heads, literally.

James, the brother of John was killed with a **machete (knife, ax, or blade).** However, there is an outstanding example of a person whose soul experienced an ax; and it was not physical. **Thus, the first resurrection can also include those who may not be martyred physically.**

Beheaded means: to chop off with an ax. The "souls" in the verses above who had part in the first resurrection experienced the ax. This also happened to Joseph who is our example that shows that even though some may not be killed physically with an ax, they will still have part in the first resurrection. Joseph experienced an ax; and Joseph appears to be among those raised after Jesus' resurrection in Matthew 27.

Psalms 105:17-18: *17He sent a man before them, even Joseph, who was sold for a servant: 18Whose feet they hurt with fetters: **he was laid in iron.***

*2 Kings 6:5: But as one was felling a beam, the **axe head** fell into the water: and he cried, and said, Alas, master! For it was borrowed.*

In Psalms 107:18b, above, the word **"he"** is the Hebrew word **"nephesh"** which literally means **"soul." "Iron"** is the same Hebrew word translated as **"axe head"** in 2 Kings 6:5. Thus, Psalms 105:18b above can read, "His **soul** was laid into an **ax head.**" Here are how some other translations read.

Psalms 105:17-18, YLT: "... **iron** hath entered his **soul.**"

Psalms 105:17-18, Darby: "... his **soul** came into **irons.**"

Psalms 105:17-18, Septuagint: "... his **soul** came into **irons.**"

Joseph experienced the "iron" of the "ax head" in his "soul." Joseph was not killed literally, yet he did experience the ax of tribulation that affected his soul.[130] Joseph (who is also a type of our Lord Jesus) is an example to those in Revelation 20:4 who will experience the ax to their soul without literal death; and they will be part of the first resurrection. What are some of the ways Joseph's soul experienced the ax?

The ax of hate—Joseph was hated[131] by his half-brothers because his father loved him as "a son of his old age," just as Jesus is the beloved Son of the Ancient of Days and was hated by the Pharisees.[132] **The ax of abandonment**—Joseph was thrown in a pit[133] by his half-brothers, just like Jesus who descended into hell for our sins.

The ax of slavery—Joseph was sold for a slave,[134] like Jesus who took on the form of a slave for us.[135] **The ax of false witnesses**[136]—Joseph was lied on by the harlot, which landed him in prison for two years, as false witness was given against Jesus who caused him to be jailed before His crucifixion.[137]

Joseph also had another similarity to this group who experienced the ax to their souls. The Word of the Lord was the catalyst for Joseph's trials. "The word of the Lord tried him (Joseph)."[138] Revelation 20:4 indicated something similar for those in the first resurrection; their souls experience the ax **"through" the witness of Jesus ("the spirit of the prophecy"), and "through" the Word of God.** As indicated above, it was the **"Word"** that also tried Joseph, the Word in the dreams the Lord gave Joseph concerning Joseph's future.

God may give you words like the ones He gave to Joseph, yet you must know that the Word of God will try your soul and cutoff (ax) all soulish[139] ways through His Word. Jesus said that the souls of the believers must be crucified (killed) to gain them.

Matthew 16:24-25: ²⁴*Then said Jesus unto his disciples, if any [man] will come after me, let him deny himself, and take up his* **cross,** *and follow me.* ²⁵ *For whosoever will save his* **life (lit., soul)** *shall lose it: and whosoever will lose his* **life (lit., soul)** *for my sake shall find it.*

In the first resurrection those whose souls were cut off by the ax found life in the first resurrection. There is a "part" for those in Christ who have allowed the testimony of Jesus (the spirit of the prophecy, or prophetic words) to crucify soulish desires.

There is a part in the first resurrection for those who allow the Word of God to bring their souls into the ax. We in Christ are not to be afraid of trial and tribulation. Tribulation (pressure) is one of the avenues by which we are counted worthy for the first resurrection. [140]

Suffering to Obtain the Resurrection "Out of" the Dead

*Hebrews 11:35: Women received their dead raised to life again: and others were tortured, not accepting deliverance; that **they might obtain (or lit., they may be happening)** a better resurrection.*

*Luke 20:35: [35]But they which shall be accounted **worthy** to **obtain that world**, and the resurrection **from** the dead, neither marry, nor are given in marriage: [36]neither can they die anymore ....*

The verses above can read as such: "...they which shall be counted worthy **'to be happening on'** that **'age'** and the resurrection **'out of'** the dead neither marry, nor are they given in marriage: **neither can they 'die off' anymore ...."**

There will be some who **"happen"** on that age who will not 'die off' anymore. Some saints will be transfigured at **"that age"** and **"neither can they die off anymore."** There will also be some who will "happen" on the resurrection **"out of"** the dead. Thus, not **all** the dead will be raised in "that age," just some "out of" the dead.

This resurrection "out-of the dead" is the partial resurrection that will take place in the first resurrection. Thus, the question must be asked, what is the qualification to "happen" upon the "part" of the first resurrection? The answer is we have to be "made conformable" to Jesus' sufferings and death.

*Philippians 3:10-11: [10]That I may know him, and the power of his resurrection, and the **fellowship of his sufferings, being made conformable unto his death;** [11]**If by any means** I might attain unto the resurrection **of (lit., out of)** the dead.*

Paul used the same phrase "the resurrection 'out of' the dead" that Jesus used in Luke 20:35. Paul also said to "attain unto the resurrection out of the dead" is linked to "sufferings" and "being made conformable unto [Jesus'] death." Paul strived for this **"fellowship of [Jesus] suffering … if by any means"** he may partake of the firstfruit resurrection. The writer of Hebrews believes the same.

There is "a better resurrection." This better resurrection is linked to accepting sufferings, knowing that you will be rewarded "before-most" in "that age" of the resurrection out of the dead. The rest of the dead will be resurrected and rewarded later.

*Hebrews 11:35: Women received their dead raised to life again: and **others were tortured, not accepting deliverance; that they might obtain (lit., that they may be happening) a better resurrection.***

The Church of today has avoided sufferings. Yet, the Bible I read says that having "part" of the "rank" of the first resurrection—the better resurrection—is linked to **"not accepting deliverance" (from torture) "that they may be happening [on] a better resurrection."**

As indicated earlier, Joseph suffered, and his bones were among those who were raised out of the dead <u>after</u> Jesus' resurrection. Our souls, like Jesus' and Joseph's, must experience the ax of suffering. Paul said that we are "appointed" to tribulations.[141]

Our "soulish" ways will be dealt with by the Holy Spirit and the Word of God. The Bible said that **"it is necessary as binding"** that through much tribulation we enter the kingdom of God.[142] This truth has not changed. Suffering persecutions and tribulations in this beastly world and from these beast systems makes us worthy of Jesus' kingdom. We can be made worthy to obtain a better resurrection out of the dead through suffering.

2 Thessalonians 1:4-5, NKJ: 4so that we ourselves boast of you among the churches of God for your patience and faith in all your ***persecutions*** *and* ***tribulations*** *that you endure, 5which is manifest evidence of the righteous judgment of God* ***that you may be counted worthy*** *of the kingdom of God, for which you also suffer.*

Resurrection for Those Who Do Not Serve the Beast

Revelation 20:4; 6: 4… I saw … which had not ***worshipped the beast,*** *neither* ***his image,*** *neither had received his mark upon their* ***foreheads,*** *or in their* ***hands;*** *and they lived and reigned with Christ a thousand years …6Blessed and holy is he that hath part in the first resurrection.*

The other qualification for being "part" of the first resurrection is that those in Christ are not supposed to worship the beast or his image. They are also not to receive the beast's mark in their forehead and on their right hand. With that said, I will not go into too much detail in this book concerning the beast, except what needs to be said to give a sound understanding as to why no human is to serve the beast system.

Simply put, the beast existed from the days of the prophet Daniel up to John, the beloved apostle; and **a** beast, its mark, its image exists today as one does in every age. Daniel saw all the beasts (kings and kingdoms) that would rule in the earth until the Stone Kingdom takes over.[143] John, the beloved also saw similar beasts that existed in his day as declared in the book of Revelations.[144]

Basically put, the beast is the systems of mankind that rule the kingdoms of men.[145] Note: the Bible does say to honor kings.[146] The Bible also said, "Submit yourselves to every ordinance of man for the Lord's sake: whether it be to the king, as supreme."[147] Yet, the same Bible also said that we are not to worship the beast (a king and a kingdom) and his image (the image of the world).

With that said, those who <u>did not</u> worship the beast had "part" in the first resurrection. Worship of the beast basically includes those who pay homage to a government's ability to make war against humanity, against Jesus' saints, and against the Lamb, Himself.[148] We are not to worship or pay homage to a system that wages war against its people or the saints. Humanity should not worship a kingdom that has the military might to be the top war machine; and thus, boasts about that ability to make war, as exemplified in Revelation 13:4. (Being prepared militarily to protect one's nation is different from ostentatious war mongering. [149]) We are also <u>not</u> to worship the image of the beast.

The beast has an image that was given breath (lit., spirit) by "another beast," the false prophet.[150] This image of the beast could both speak and cause people who did not worship the beast's image to be killed. Today, image is everything. There is an image of this beastly world, and some in the Church are ruled by this image. It is the "unclean spirit" out of the false prophet's mouth that gave "breath" to this worldly image that will kill any who cannot worship or keep up with its worldly image.[151]

Some in the Church are now controlled by the image of the beast. The conspicuous consumption of the beast system has become the image that preachers and saints alike mimic. The antichrist image of the world has become the standard to conform to, rather than being conformed to the image of the invisible God—Jesus. To partake of the first resurrection, beast-image worship must <u>not</u> exist in the Church of Jesus.

Next, to partake of the first resurrection, one must **not** receive the mark of the beast in one's forehead or hand. Again, for the sake of simplicity, the mark of the beast is the "character" of the beast. Mark is the Greek word "charagma" which means character, expressed image, exact representation, and so on. Thus, for one to partake in the first resurrection, one cannot receive the character of the beast, which is (666) man's complete "hindering" of Jesus' "fame."

Here is a question, which do most believers of today act like, wild beasts or Christ? Does the beast's character dominate one's life, or does the character of Christ dominate? To be part of the first resurrection, the mark (character) of the beast cannot be found on a person's forehead (how one sees and thinks), and the character of the beast cannot be found on one's hands (what's done with one's hands).

The mark of the beast in the hands of men can mean people who steal with their hands; people who kill with their hands; people who rape with their hands, people who make dumb idols, and so on. The mark of the beast in the forehead points to people who allow the beast system to change the proper way to see Jesus' love for us. The mark of the beast in one's forehead is also an inability to repent (change one's mind).

Forehead literally means, between the eyes, beyond the eyes or to change the eyes. What is beyond the forehead? The mind! What does it mean to "change the eye" with the beast's character? It means that the mark or character of the beast has the ability, in a negative way, to change the way people "see" Jesus and God, the Father. The beast and the false prophet have a way of blaspheming Jesus; that is, the beast and his image have a way of hindering the fame of Jesus. 152

To be part of the firstfruit resurrection or the first resurrection, one must overcome beast worship. One must overcome image worship and overcome the beast. **It is possible to victoriously come out of the acts of the beast and the acts of its worship.**

*Revelation 15:2-4, NIV: ²And I saw what looked like a sea of glass mixed with fire and, standing beside the sea, **those who had been victorious over the beast and his image and over the number of his name.** They held harps given them by God ³and sang the song of Moses the servant of God and the song of the Lamb: "Great and marvelous are your deeds, Lord God Almighty. Just and true are your ways, King of the ages. ⁴Who will not fear you, O Lord, and bring glory to your name? For you alone are holy. All nations will come and worship before you, **for your righteous acts have been revealed."***

With that said, there are some that put the beast and his mark as future; however, the Bibles I read, which is probably the same Bibles they read (KJV, NKJ, NIV, NAU, etc.) explicitly indicate that the beast and is mark is a present reality in every age, including these days. Thus, saints must be careful not to lose their part in the first resurrection by partaking of the beast.

Remember that John *"⁴ ... saw thrones, and they sat upon them, and judgment was given unto them: and [John] saw the souls of them that were beheaded for the witness of Jesus, and for the word of God, **and which (lit., and any who)** had not worshipped the beast, neither his image, neither had received his mark upon their foreheads, or in their hands; and **they lived and reigned with Christ a thousand years.** ⁵But the rest of the dead lived not again until the thousand years were finished. This is the first resurrection. ⁶Blessed and holy is he that hath part in the first resurrection: on such the second death hath no power, but they shall be priests of God and of Christ and shall reign with him a thousand years"* **(Revelation 20:4-6).**

The Dead in Christ Will Rise First

---

*1 Thessalonians 4:14-17, NKJ: ¹⁴For if we believe that Jesus died and rose again, even so God will bring with **Him those who sleep in Jesus.** ¹⁵For this we say to you by the word of the Lord, that we who* *are alive and remain until **the coming of the Lord** will by no means precede those who are asleep.* ¹⁶*For the Lord Himself will descend from heaven with a shout, with the voice of an archangel, and with the trumpet of God.* ***And the dead in Christ will rise first.*** ¹⁷*Then we who are alive and remain shall be caught up together with them in the clouds to meet the Lord in the air. And thus, we shall always be with the Lord.*

The debate concerning who will rise in the first resurrection is settled in one person—Jesus. **"Those also who sleep 'through' Jesus"** will God bring with Him; and in the coming of the Lord **"The dead in Christ will rise first."** Therefore, the groups that were described in Revelation 20:4-5 included people who are in Christ, since they are described as "the first resurrection. Paul said the dead "in Christ" shall rise first; and John said that "this is the first resurrection" when referring to the group in Revelation 20:4-5. Therefore, if any man is not "in Christ," they will not partake of the first resurrection. Saying it another way, only those who choose to be in Christ by accepting the invitation of God to believe **into Jesus Christ** will rise first.

Galatians 3:26-28, NKJ: ²⁶*For you are all sons of God through faith in Christ Jesus.* ²⁷***For as many of you as were baptized into Christ have put on Christ.*** ²⁸*There is neither Jew nor Greek, there is neither slave nor free, there is neither male nor female; **for you are all one in Christ Jesus**.*

If you want to partake of the first resurrection in either phase, you must have faith in Christ Jesus and must be baptized into Christ with the baptism of the Holy Spirit. We "put on Christ" by the baptism of the Holy Spirit. That is, we become "in Christ" if we "put on Christ." It is written, "Now if anyone does not have the Spirit of Christ, he is not His." We must be baptized into Christ (Head and Body—Jesus and His Church) through the Holy Spirit. *"For by one Spirit we were all baptized into one body."*

1 Corinthians 12:12, NKJ: [12] *For as the body is one and has many members, but all the members of that one body, being many, are one body, so also is Christ.* [13] ***For by one Spirit we were all baptized into one body** -- whether Jews or Greeks, whether slaves or free -- and have all been made to drink into one Spirit.*

Galatians 5:24, NKJ: And those who are Christ's have crucified the flesh with its passions and desires.

*Romans 8:9, NKJ: But you are not in the flesh but in the Spirit, if indeed the Spirit of God dwells in you. **Now if anyone does not have the Spirit of Christ, he is not His.***

So, here is the simplicity "in Christ" concerning the first resurrection. To rise first, or to be a part of the first resurrection one must be "in Christ." Being in Christ also means to be baptized by the Holy Spirit into the one Body of Christ. They that are Christ's have crucified the flesh with its "emotions" and lusts. This crucifixion of the flesh is only possible through the Spirit of Christ that God has sent forth into our hearts; and first resurrection out of the dead is only possible for those in Christ through the Spirit of God.

*Romans 8:11, NKV: But if **the Spirit of Him who raised Jesus** from the dead dwells in you, He who raised Christ from the dead will also give life to your mortal bodies **through His Spirit** who dwells in you.*

Romans 1:3-4, NKJ: [3]*concerning His Son Jesus Christ our Lord, who was born of the seed of David according to the flesh,* [4]*and declared to be the Son of God with power **according to the Spirit of holiness, by the resurrection from the dead.***

*Revelation 11:11: And after three days and a half the **Spirit of life** from God entered into them, **and they stood upon their feet;** and great fear fell upon them which saw them.*

The Coming of Our Lord Jesus

*2 Peter 1:16: For we have not followed cunningly devised fables, when we made known unto you the power and **coming of our Lord Jesus Christ but** were eyewitnesses of his majesty.*

It appears to me that one of the most misunderstood topics is the physical "coming" of our Lord Jesus from heaven. I have also misunderstood it. It also appears that the heavenly Father deliberately did not make the "times and seasons" of His coming clear and easy to be understood.[153] Some have invented words like **"the rapture"** to falsely predict Jesus' coming at "any minute," and skipped a process in the resurrection of the dead.

There is no such word ("rapture") in the Bible, or in the Strong's Exhaustive Concordance. The phrase "the rapture" is found in either? So then, when is Jesus' physical coming?

With that said, the Bible does give us a hint of the "times and seasons"[154] of His coming. It is found in the most unlikely book of the Bible. I say the most unlikely book because the apostle that authored the book was not necessarily a scholar like Paul. This apostle's name is Peter.

Peter Eye Witnessed Jesus' Coming

In 2 Peter, Apostle Peter declared that he had made known to the believers he was writing to, "the power and **coming of our Lord Jesus.**" Peter did not stop there. He also said that he was an **"eyewitness"** of His majesty — the "majesty" of the power and **coming** of our Lord Jesus.

Thus, a logical question is: when did Peter see the coming of our Lord Jesus? Peter gave the answer in 2 Peter 1:18. That is, Peter equated Jesus' transfiguration in the holy mountain as Jesus His coming. Let us look at the verses.

Page | 73

2 Peter 1:16-18: ¹⁶*For we have not followed cunningly devised fables, when we made known unto you the* **power and coming of our Lord Jesus Christ but** *were* **eyewitnesses** *of his majesty.* ¹⁷*For he received from God the Father honor and glory, when there came such a voice to him from the excellent glory, this is my beloved Son, in whom I am well pleased.* ¹⁸*And this voice which came from heaven we heard when* **we were with him in the holy mount.**

Let us go through the verses again for clarity. In 2 Peter 1:16, Peter declared that he made known to the believers he was writing to "the power and **coming of our Lord Jesus Christ,"** and that he was an **"eyewitness"** of Jesus' coming. In the subsequent verses of 2 Peter 1:18, Peter explained that he and others saw this "coming of our Lord Jesus Christ" when they **"were with him in the holy mount."**

This was the same time that Peter also said that he heard God's voice speak to Jesus in the holy mount. Thus, 2 Peter 2:16-18, provides explicit understanding concerning the coming of the Lord Jesus Christ. So much so, that Peter was able to **"make known"** unto the saints the "coming of the Lord Jesus."

Thus, **we** (present day believers) can also **"know"** the power and coming of the Lord. How can the saints of today "know" the power and coming of the Lord Jesus Christ? We can know by looking at the same event Peter equated to the Lord's coming in what Peter "saw" and "heard."

In other words, from the experience on the mountain where Jesus was transfigured, we can know as Peter made known to the Church, the Lord's coming. Since, Peter's account of the power and coming of the Lord Jesus is the account of what he experienced when Jesus was transfigured. Let us compare some of the other disciples (Matthew, Mark, and Luke's) accounts with Peter's account of the same experience of the coming of our Lord Jesus Christ.

Jesus' Transfiguration, the Pattern of His Coming

Matthew 16:28-17:1-6: *16:28Verily I say unto you, there be some standing here, which shall not taste of death, till they **see the Son of man coming in his kingdom.** 17:1And after six days Jesus taketh Peter, James, and John his brother, and brings them up into a high mountain apart, 17:2And was **transfigured** before them: and his face did shine as the sun, and his raiment was white as the light. 17:3And, behold, there appeared unto them Moses and Elias talking with him. 17:4Then answered Peter, and said unto Jesus, Lord, it is good for us to be here: if you wilt, let us make here three tabernacles; one for thee, and one for Moses, and one for Elias. 17:5While he yet spoke, behold, a bright cloud overshadowed them: **and behold a voice out of the cloud, which said, this is my beloved Son, in whom I am well pleased; hear you him.** 17:6And when the disciples heard it, they fell on their face, and were sore afraid.*

Mark 9:1-7: *1And he said unto them, Verily I say unto you, that there be some of them that stand here, which shall not taste of death, till they have seen the kingdom of God come with power. 2And after six days Jesus taketh with him Peter, and James, and John, and leads them up into a high mountain apart by themselves: and he was **transfigured before them.** 3And his raiment became shining, exceeding white as snow; so, as no **'cloth-dresser'** on earth can white them. 4And there appeared unto them Elias with Moses: and they were talking with Jesus. 5And Peter answered and said to Jesus, Master, it is good for us to be here: and let us make three tabernacles; one for thee, and one for Moses, and one for Elias. 6For he [know] not what to say; for they were sore afraid. 7**And there was a cloud that overshadowed them: and a voice came out of the cloud, saying, this is my beloved Son: hear him.***

Luke 9:27-35: *27But I tell you of a truth, there be some standing here, which shall not taste of death, till they see the kingdom of God.*

²⁸And it came to pass about **eight days** after these sayings, he took Peter and John and James, and went up into a mountain to pray. ²⁹And as he prayed, **the fashion of his countenance was altered,** and his raiment was white and glistering. ³⁰And, behold, there talked with him two men, which were Moses and Elias: ³¹Who appeared in glory, and spoke of his decease which he should accomplish at Jerusalem. ³²But Peter and they that were with him were heavy with sleep: and when they were awake, they saw his glory, and the two men that stood with him. ³³And it came to pass, as they departed from him, Peter said unto Jesus, Master, it is good for us to be here: and let us make three tabernacles; one for thee, and one for Moses, and one for Elias: not knowing what he said. ³⁴While he thus spoke, there came a cloud, and overshadowed them: and they feared as they entered into the cloud. ³⁵**And there came a voice out of the cloud, saying, this is my beloved Son: hear him.**

2 Peter 1:16-18: ¹⁶For we have not followed cunningly devised fables, when we made known unto you the power and coming of our Lord Jesus Christ but were eyewitnesses of his majesty. ¹⁷For he received from God the Father honor and glory, **when there came such a voice** to him from the excellent glory, **this is my beloved Son, in whom I am well pleased.** ¹⁸And this voice which came from heaven we heard when we were with him in the holy mount.

Now that we have read all the accounts of the Lord's **transfiguration,** which **Peter calls Jesus' "coming,"** let us look at the same references with only the points that Peter highlighted for simplicity.

Matthew 16:28-17:1-5: ¹⁶:²⁸Verily I say unto you, there be some standing here, which shall not taste of death, till they **see the Son of man coming** in his kingdom ... ²... And was transfigured before them ... ⁵... a bright cloud overshadowed them: and behold a voice out of the cloud, which said, this is my beloved Son, in whom I am well pleased; hear you him.

Mark 9:1-7: *[1]And he said unto them, Verily I say unto you, that there be some of them that stand here, which shall not taste of death,* **till they have seen the kingdom of God come with power** ... *and he was transfigured before them ... [7]And there was a cloud that overshadowed them: and a voice came out of the cloud, saying, this is my beloved Son: hear him.*

Luke 9:27-35: *[27]But I tell you of a truth, there be some standing here, which shall not taste of death,* **till they see the kingdom of God** ... *And as he prayed, the fashion of his countenance was altered, and ...[34]While he thus spoke, there came a cloud, and overshadowed them ...[35]And there came a voice out of the cloud, saying, this is my beloved Son: hear him.*

2 Peter 1:16-18: *[16]For we have not followed cunningly devised fables, when we made known unto you the* **power and coming of our Lord Jesus Christ but** *were eyewitnesses of his majesty. [17]For he received from God the Father honor and glory, when there came such a voice to him from the excellent glory, this is my beloved Son, in whom I am well pleased. [18]And this voice which came from heaven we heard when we were with him in the holy mount.*

Peter's account is the same as Matthew, Mark, and Luke's. They saw Jesus transfigured (Jesus became gloried before their eyes), as Moses and Elijah also appeared with Jesus "in glory" — Luke 9:31). This transfiguration of Jesus (Jesus' gloried state) is what Peter called Jesus' **"coming."** In Matthew's account, Jesus Himself called His transfiguration "the Son of Man **coming** in His kingdom." In Luke's account this transfiguration is seeing the Kingdom of God. That is, the Kingdom of God is linked to Jesus' coming.

Thus, Peter also used the word **"power"** relative to Jesus coming when he recounted his experience on the holy mount. Peter got this from the Lord, because the Lord Jesus called His transfiguration the "power" of His kingdom. The Lord said in Mark's account, "Verily I say unto you, that there be some of them that **stand here,** which shall not taste of death, till they have seen **the kingdom of God** come 'in' **power."**

Peter said that "we (Peter, James and John) heard" God's voice say that Jesus is God's beloved Son, in Whom God is well pleased. Matthew, Mark, and Luke gave the same account. They all stated that the voice of God spoke, and said that Jesus is His Beloved Son, in Whom He is well pleased.

If this truth that Jesus' transfiguration prefigures His coming is understood, as outlined above, then you are ready for the next layer of truth concerning the coming of our Lord Jesus Christ. Peter's account of the transfiguration is called Jesus' power and coming. Thus, if one reads the gospel of Matthew, Mark, and Luke, the approximate "times and seasons" (plural) of Jesus' coming can also be extrapolated.

After Six (6) Days, About Eight (8) Days

Matthew 16:28-17:1-2: [16:28]*Verily I say unto you, there be some standing here, which shall not taste of death, till they see the Son of man coming in his kingdom.*[17:1]***And after six days*** *Jesus taketh Peter, James, and John his brother, and brings them up into a high mountain apart,* [17: 2] *And was transfigured before them ....*

Mark 9:1-7: [1]*And he said unto them, Verily I say unto you, that there be some of them that stand here, which shall not taste of death, till they have seen the kingdom of God come with power.* [2]***And after six days*** *Jesus taketh with him Peter, and James, and John, and leads them up into a high mountain apart by themselves: and he was* ***transfigured before them.***

Luke 9:27-29: [27]*But I tell you of a truth, there be some standing here, which shall not taste of death, till they see the kingdom of God.* [28]***And it came to pass about eight days*** *after these sayings, he took Peter and John and James, and went up into a mountain to*

pray. [29]And as he prayed, the fashion of his countenance was altered
....

In the account above that prefigures Jesus' coming, all three gospels gave the time when the **transfiguration (Jesus' power and coming)** took place. Matthew and Mark said that it was **"after six days."** Luke said that it happened **"about eight days after"** Jesus declared that they would not die until they see His coming.

Thus, the event of Jesus' transfiguration happened after six days, or around eight days after Jesus made His comment. Jesus stated that there were "some" (Peter, James, and John) standing with Him would see the coming of His kingdom. They did indeed see the kingdom come before they died. They saw it after six (6) to eight (8) days later.

The phrases **"after six days" "about eight days"** may prophetically point to thousands of years also. Six days can also equate to six thousand years. Eight days can also represent eight thousand years. Peter declared **"that one day is with the Lord as a thousand years, and a thousand years as one day."**[155]

Peter's principle of the thousand years-day principle provides <u>some</u> understanding into the plan of God concerning Jesus' coming. According to 2 Peter 1:16-18, the whole transfiguration experience prefigures Jesus' coming. Thus, the **approximate** times and seasons of Jesus' coming can also be understood. According to Paul, the coming of the Lord will occur in the times and seasons of the night, yet Jesus coming is called "day." In addition, Paul also said "the day of the Lord" will not overtake us (surprise us) like a thief in the night. Only the unbelievers will be surprised by the coming of the Lord, not the sons of light, or the sons of the day.

1 Thessalonians 4:15 - 5:5, NAU: *[15]For this we say to you by the word of the Lord, that we who are alive and remain **until the coming of the Lord,** will not precede those who have fallen asleep. [16]For the Lord Himself will descend from heaven with a shout, with the voice of the archangel and with the trumpet of God, and the dead in Christ will rise first. [17]Then we who are alive and remain will be caught up together with them in the clouds to meet the Lord in the air, and so we shall always be with the Lord. [18]Therefore comfort one another with these words. [5:1]Now **as to the times and the epochs,** brethren, you have no need of anything to be written to you. [2]For you yourselves know full well that the day of the Lord will come **just like a thief in the night....** [4]But you, brethren, are not in darkness, that the day would overtake you like a thief ....*

With the Lord, One Day is as One Thousand Years

*2 Peter 3:8, NIV: But do not forget this one thing, dear friends: With the Lord **a day is like a thousand years**, and a thousand years are like a day.*

*Matthew 17:1-2: And **after six days** Jesus ...was transfigured before them ....*

*Luke 9:28-29: And ... **about eight days** after these sayings ... as he prayed, the fashion of his countenance was altered ....*

First, let us establish that Jesus first physical coming was at the beginning of the fourth (4th) millennium after the first Adam. We are now approximately six (6) millennia from the first Adam, or two (2) millennia from when Jesus (the last Adam) came. We are about to begin the seventh (7th) millennium from the first Adam, or the third (3rd) millennium from Jesus' death, burial, and resurrection.

With the above said, and before we use Peter's thousand years-day principle with the verses above, let us look at the details again just for clarity. It was after six (6) days that Jesus was transfigured, according to Matthew and Mark. What day comes after the sixth (6th) day? That would be the seventh (7th) day. Thus, the transfiguration happened some time **"after"** day six.

In addition, Luke's account, according to the Greek texts, is also rich with truth. Luke said that Jesus' transfiguration took place "**about** eight days." Thus, this is agreeable, because the eighth (8th) day is indeed "after six days." The truth shows that Jesus did not transfigure (a type of His coming) on the sixth (day), He was transfigured after the sixth (6th) day.

Thus, all who were declaring that Jesus would come any minute, before the end of this sixth millennium from the first Adam, were incomplete in their teachings. How do we know that their "rapture" prediction is incomplete? First, Jesus did not come as they erroneously prophesied.

Second, we are just at the close of the sixth (6th) day (6,000 years) from the first Adam; and Jesus was transfigured **"after"** the sixth (6th) day, not before. This says to me that the coming of our Lord Jesus Christ can happen **"after"** the six thousand years (6000) from the first Adam, and there is also a significant "coming" related to the eighth millennium. One prophetic week (7 days) can be equated to seven thousand years-days; thus, the eighth millennium would point to the start of a new prophetic week.

Thus, Jesus' physical coming in His flesh and bone form (the same way He went to heaven) may probably be after the completion of this sixth millennium from the first Adam. We are approximately six days from the first Adam, or according to Peter's thousand years-day principle; we are approximately six thousand (6,000) years from Adam and Eve. We are at the close of the sixth millennium from the first Adam. We are in the overlap between the sixth and seventh millennium. It also seems that there will be a significant coming of the Lord about the eighth day as this coming relates coming to God inhabiting the temple of God by His Spirit. Remember Paul indicated that the coming of the Lord is related to "times (plural) and seasons (plural)."

Thus, if Matthew and Mark's accounts are correct—and they are—the Scriptures cannot be broken. And if Luke's account is correct—and it is—then this Scripture also cannot be voided. **What is a revelation of the two accounts— "after six days," "about eight days?"** If we follow Matthew and Mark's account Jesus can indeed come **"after"** six thousand years from the first Adam. If we follow Luke's account, Jesus can indeed come about the eighth day, as the Church would have been built for a permanent habitation of God through the Spirit[156] at the millennium's end.

The Coming of the Lord after Six Days

The millennium rule of the resurrected saints with Christ seems to be related to the commencement of the seventh millennium. Since, it appears that the Lord will come **after** the sixth millennium from Adam; there must be an overlap[1] between the end of the sixth millennium and the beginning of the seventh millennium. The time of the overlap is between the seventh or last trumpet and the beginning of the millennium reign of Christ and the saints <u>with</u> Him. This principle of an overlap between the ages can be seen in Goliath.

Goliath is a type of the man of sin, and the effect of the number and mark of the beast. Goliath, the offspring of the

---

[1] Please refer to the chapter titled "The Overlap" in one of my other books titled, *The Last Hour, the First Hour, The 42nd Generation.*

giants had a height of six cubits and a span[157]. His height of six cubits points to six thousand years from Adam during which the arrogance of man ruled, and the "span"[158] points to the overlap of his influence, the time when his forehead (one of the places of the mark of the beast) was stoned to death. Thus, in the season of the overlap, Jesus destroys the beast with the appearing of His coming and the Spirit of His mouth. With that said, let us look at some Scriptures that demonstrate that the Lord may come during the "seventh trumpet," which is the same trumpet as the "last trumpet," which is also called the "trumpet of God."

He Who Comes Before the Millennium Reign

Revelation 1:4: John to the seven churches which are in Asia: Grace be unto you, and peace, from him which is, and which was, and **which is to come**....

Revelation 1:4, English Majority Text Version (EMTV): John, to the seven churches which are in Asia: Grace be to you and peace from Him who is, and who was, and **who is to come**....

Revelation 1:8: I am Alpha and Omega, the beginning, and the ending, says the Lord, which is, and which was, and **which is to come,** *the Almighty.*

Revelation 1:8, English Majority Text Version (EMTV): "I am the Alpha and Omega," says the Lord God, the beginning He who is and who was, and **He who is to come,** *The Almighty.*

Revelation 4:8: And the four beasts ... rest not day and night, saying, Holy, holy, holy, Lord God Almighty, which was, and is, and **is to come.**

Revelation 4:8, English Majority Text Version (EMTV): And the living beings ... never rest day or night, saying, Holy, holy, holy, Lord God Almighty, He who was, and who is, and **is to who is to come.**

*Revelation 11:17: ... We give thee thanks, O Lord God Almighty, which art, and was, **and are to come,** because you have taken to thee thy great power ....*

*Revelation 11:17, English Majority Text Version (EMTV): ... We give you thanks, O Lord God Almighty, **the One who is and who was,** because You have taken Your great power ....*

*Revelation 11:17, NAU: ... "We give You thanks, O Lord God, the Almighty, **who are and who were,** because You have taken Your great power ....*

In the verses above with regards to the King James Version, we see the phrases that indicate that the Lord Almighty "was," "is" and **"is to come."** However, the King James Version is only translated from one (1) text, while the Majority Texts is translated from over five thousand (5,000) texts. The New American Standard Bible (updated version) was translated from the Alexandrian Texts. With that said, in Revelation 11:17, in all the manuscripts except for one, they all excluded the phrase "who is to come."

It seems to me that five thousand (5,000) texts should be considered more dependable than one (1) "Received Text." Yet with that said, the King James Version written from the "Received Text" is my favorite version and the version that I read, meditate from and study from. So, this is not a discredit to the King James Bible, but a clarification for the sake of the truth.

Again, with regards to the verses listed above, the majority of the Greek manuscripts indeed does say **"He is to come"** until we get to Revelation 11:17. In Revelation 11:17, "He is to come" is not mentioned anymore; and Revelation 11:17 is to occur during the seventh trumpet. Again, Paul defined this seventh trumpet as the "last trumpet," and the "trump of God."

That is, when the seventh trumpet sounds, the phrase **"He who is to come"** is not in the oldest Greek texts. The oldest texts excluded the phrase "to come;" because "the coming of the Lord will be "in" the "days of the seventh trumpet" which Paul also calls the "last trumpet" So, it appears to me that the phrase "He who is to come" is excluded from Revelation 11:17 because the seventh (or last) trumpet is related to the "times and seasons" when the Lord Jesus comes.

In other words, there is no need to say "He is to come" if the Lord comes during the seventh trumpet. According to Paul, in his first book to the Thessalonians, the Lord comes during the **"trumpet of God." At which time,** the dead in Christ first will be the first to rise. And according to, 1 Corinthians 15:51-52, the resurrection related to inheriting the kingdom of God occurs in the **last trumpet**. It follows that the same is true for the seventh trumpet (the last of the seven trumpets).

*1 Thessalonians 4:15-16: NKJ: ¹⁵For ... we who are alive and remain until the coming of the Lord will by no means precede those who are asleep. ¹⁶For the Lord Himself will descend from heaven ... **with the trumpet of God.** And the dead in Christ will rise first.*

*1 Corinthians 15:51-52, NKJ: ⁵¹Behold, I tell you a mystery: We shall not all sleep, but we shall all be changed -- ⁵²in a moment, in the twinkling of an eye, **at the last trumpet.** For the **trumpet will sound,** and **the dead will be raised incorruptible,** and we shall be changed.*

*Revelation 11:15-17, NIV: ¹⁵The **seventh angel sounded his trumpet** .... ¹⁶And the twenty-four elders ... worshiped God, ¹⁷saying: "We give thanks to you, Lord God Almighty, the One who is and who was, because you have taken your **great power** and have begun to reign.*

All three of the texts above agree in heralding the coming of the Lord. In His coming, the "trumpet of God" will sound and the dead in Christ will rise first. The "last trumpet" will sound, and the dead will be raised incorruptible. The seventh trumpet sounded, and no mention of the Lord's future coming occurs because He appears to come during the seventh trumpet, and resurrection also occurred being understood by the using of the phrase His "great power," which will be discussed shortly.

So, lets us review again. The Lord comes during the times and seasons of the seventh trumpet. Therefore, His is no longer referred to as "He who is to come," because he apparently will come during the seventh trumpet. This theme of the exclusion of His coming, after the seventh trumpet sounded, continues in Revelation 16 in all the Greek texts except for the one used to translate the King James Bible.

*Revelation 16:5, NAU: And I heard the angel of the waters saying, "Righteous are You, **who are and who were**, O Holy One, because You judged these things.*

*Revelation 16:5, EMTV: And I heard the angel of the waters saying: "You are Righteous, **who is and who was**, holy, because You have judged these things.*

*Revelation 16:5, NIV: Then I heard the angel in charge of the waters say: "You are just in these judgments, O Holy One, **you who are and who were.***

The theme that He "is" and that He "was" continues here with no mention that He "is to come." Why? He appears to come during the seventh trumpet that sounded in Revelation 11. Revelation 11 also hinted that during the seventh (the last of seven) trumpet there will be resurrection involved.

*Revelation 11:15; 17, EMTV: And the **seventh angel sounded his trumpet;** and there were great voices in heaven, saying, "The kingdoms of this world has become the kingdoms of our Lord, and of*

*His Christ; and He shall reign forever and ever…. We give you thanks, O Lord God Almighty, **the One who is and who was,** because You have taken Your **great power**, and have begun to reign.*

*Acts 4:33: And with **great power** gave the apostles **witness of the resurrection of the Lord Jesus: and** great grace was upon them all.*

During the sounding of the seventh angel with his seventh trumpet, the Lord will be worshipped for taking His "great power," and He will also be worshipped for His reign. What is this "great power?" According to the book of Acts, God's "great power" is associated with Jesus' resurrection power. "With **great power** gave the apostles **witness of the resurrection of the Lord Jesus**."

In 1 Thessalonians 4:13-18, we learn that a trumpet will sound and there will be resurrection in Jesus' coming. In 1 Corinthians 15:52, we also learn that the trumpet mentioned in Thessalonians is the "last trumpet." In the book of Revelation, there are seven trumpets; therefore, the seventh trumpet of the seven trumpets in the book of Revelation is the last trumpet. In the seventh trumpet, God's "great power" is in the worship of the living creatures and the twenty-four elders.

That is, it appears that during the seventh trumpet, the Lord comes, and resurrection occurs during His coming. He took "His great power" of resurrection and ruled. As a result, there is no need for the elders and the living creatures to say in their worship that Jesus is to come, because He must have come during the seventh trumpet. Now that we have reviewed this truth, and in continuation of discussing Jesus' coming before the millennium rule; let us now look at another facet of His possible coming before the millennium as King of Kings and Lord of Lords.

1 Timothy 6:13-15, NAU: *[13]I charge you in the presence of God, who gives life to all things, and of Christ Jesus, who testified the good confession before Pontius Pilate, [14]that you keep the commandment without stain or reproach until* **the appearing** *of our Lord Jesus Christ, [15]which He will bring about at the proper time-- He who is the blessed and only Sovereign,* **the King of kings and Lord of lords**

2 Thessalonians 2:8, NAU: *Then that lawless one will be revealed whom the Lord will slay with the* **breath (lit. Spirit)** *of His mouth and bring to an end by* **the appearance of His coming.**

Revelation 19:11-16, NAU: *[11]And I saw heaven opened, and behold, a white horse, and He who sat on it is called Faithful and True, and in righteousness He judges and wages war. [12]His eyes are a flame of fire, and on His head are many diadems; and He has a name written on Him which no one knows except Himself. [13]He is clothed with a robe dipped in blood, and His name is called The Word of God. [14] And the armies which are in heaven, clothed in fine linen, white and clean, were following Him on white horses. [15]From His mouth comes a sharp sword, so that with it He may strike down the nations, and He will rule them with a rod of iron; and He treads the wine press of the fierce wrath of God, the Almighty. [16]And on His robe and on His thigh, He has a name written,* **"KING OF KINGS, AND LORD OF LORDS."**

There are places in the Bible where the **"appearing" (lit., epiphany)** of the Lord points to His physical coming to the earth approximately two thousand years ago (2 Timothy 1:10). His future coming is also associated with His appearing, or epiphany; therefore, the appearing of His coming must also be physical.

2 Timothy 1:8-10: *[8]Be not you therefore ashamed of the testimony of our Lord, nor of me his prisoner: but be you partaker of the afflictions of the gospel according to the power of God; ⁹Who hath saved us, and called us with an holy calling, not according to our works, but according to his own purpose and grace, which was given us in Christ Jesus before the world began, ¹⁰But is now made manifest by the* **appearing (lit., epiphany)** *of our Savior Jesus Christ, who hath abolished death, and hath brought life and immortality to light through the gospel:*

*Titus 2:13-14: ¹³***Looking for** *that blessed hope, and the glorious* **appearing (lit., epiphany)** *of the great God and our Savior Jesus Christ; ¹⁴Who gave himself for us, that he might redeem us from all iniquity, and purify unto himself a peculiar people, zealous of good works.*

2 Thessalonians 2:8: And then shall that Wicked be revealed, whom the Lord shall consume with the spirit of his mouth, and shall destroy with the **brightness (lit., epiphany)** *of his coming:*

In 2 Timothy 1:10 we see that Jesus' first appearance (lit., epiphany) was physical. It follows that the "'epiphany; of His coming" will also be literal as "King of kings and Lord of lords," keeping in mind that this appearing as King of kings happens before the millennium rule of Christ and the resurrected saints **with Him**. This appearing is associated with Jesus manifesting that He is the **"only 'dynasty',"** **King of kings and Lord of lords**.

In other words, the phrase stating that Jesus is "King of kings and Lord of lords" used in 1 Timothy in regard to His coming, is only found in the book of Revelation in the reverse order as "Lord of lords and King of kings" (Revelation 17:14) and in Revelation 19:11-21 as "King of kings and Lord of lords." The latter is when the beast and his armies gathered to make war against Jesus and Jesus' army. And I must note here that it is in the season when the dragon, the beast and the false prophet were recruiting the kings of the earth for their battle against the Lord, that Jesus said, "behold I come as a thief." So, Jesus is scheduled to come as a thief (only to unbelievers, etc.) before the next millennium. Yet, the Father deliberately hides the exact day of Jesus coming from His people.[159]

1 Timothy 6:13-15, NAU: *[13]I charge you in the presence of God, who gives life to all things, and of Christ Jesus, who testified the good confession before Pontius Pilate, [14]that you keep the commandment without stain or reproach until **the appearing** of our Lord Jesus Christ, [15]which He will bring about at the proper time-- He who is the blessed and only Sovereign, **the King of kings and Lord of lords***

Revelation 16:13-16: *[13]And I saw three unclean spirits like frogs coming out of the mouth of the dragon, out of the mouth of the beast, and out of the mouth of the false prophet. [14]For they are spirits of demons, performing signs, which go out to **the kings of the earth and of the whole world, to gather them to the battle of that great day of God Almighty.** [15]"Behold, I am coming as a thief. Blessed is he who watches, and keeps his garments, lest he walk naked, and they see his shame." [16]And they gathered them together to the place called in Hebrew, Armageddon.*

Revelation 19:11-16; 19-20, NAU: *[11]And I saw heaven opened, and behold, a white horse, and He who sat on it is called Faithful and True, and in righteousness He judges and wages war. [12]His eyes are a flame of fire, and on His head are many diadems; and He has a name written on Him which no one knows except Himself. [13]He is clothed with a robe dipped in blood, and His name is called The Word of God. [14]And the armies which are in heaven, clothed in fine linen, white and clean, were following Him on white horses. [15] From His mouth comes a sharp sword, so that with it He may strike down the nations, and He will rule them with a rod of iron; and He treads the wine press of the fierce wrath of God, the Almighty. [16]And on His robe and on His thigh, He has a name written, **"KING OF KINGS, AND LORD OF LORDS .... And I saw the beast and the kings of the earth, and their armies assembled to make war against Him who sat on the horse and against His army.***

²⁰And the beast was seized, and with him the false prophet who performed the signs in his presence, by which he deceived those who had received the mark of the beast and those who worshiped his image; these two were thrown alive into the lake of fire which burns with brimstone.

It seems to me if we are to remain consistent with interpreting the Scriptures, as best we can, through the Holy Spirit, then Paul's reference to Jesus being recognized in his own seasons as King of kings and Lord of lords should be interpreted in the context of Revelation 19:11-20. That is, Jesus being recognized as King of kings and Lord of lords in Revelation 19:16 is related to what Paul calls his "appearing," or "the appearing of His coming" in 1 Timothy 6:13-16 and 2Thessalonians 2:8. Yet some may say, "Revelation 19:11-20 never said that Jesus **came** down from heaven on His white horse."

Though this statement may seem plausible, if one investigates the Greek text, he/she will see that the word "seized" (NAU) or "taken" (KJV) is a Greek word that also means to be pressed down by the hoof (see Liddell-Scott dictionary). Therefore, it is also plausible to say that Jesus' white horse and the other horses of His army may have descended upon the beast and the false prophet and "pressed them by the hoofs" as the beast and the false prophet were "arrested" to be judged and sent to the lake of fire — the Second Death.

Remember, I just showed above that at the season when the dragon, the beast and the false prophet were recruiting the kings of the earth for their battle against the Lord, that Jesus said, "behold I come as a thief." So, Jesus is scheduled to come as a thief (only to unbelievers) during the season when the dragon, the beast and the false prophet gather the kings of the earth and their armies to fight against Jesus. Yet, as previously stated, the Father deliberately hides the exact day of Jesus coming from His people.[160]

With that said, there are also similarities between the coming of the Lord as Paul and John called the Lord King of kings in His appearing. John's writing in some areas seems to be hidden, only to be revealed by the Holy Spirit. That is, the Holy Spirit will give understanding to spiritual truth by comparing spiritual things with spiritual things (or Scriptures with Scriptures).

*1 Thessalonians 4:16, NKJ: For the Lord Himself will descend from heaven with a shout, with the **voice of an archangel,** and with the **trumpet of God.** And the dead in Christ will rise first.*

*Revelation 19:11-17: ¹¹Now I saw heaven opened, and behold, a white horse. And He who sat on him was called Faithful and True, and in righteousness He judges and makes war. ¹² His eyes were like a flame of fire, and on His head were many crowns. He had a name written that no one knew except Himself ....¹⁶And He has on His robe and on His thigh a name written: KING OF KINGS AND LORD OF LORDS. ¹⁷Then I saw **an angel** standing in the sun; and **he cried with a loud voice,** saying to all the birds that fly in the middle of heaven, "Come and gather together for the supper of the great God.*

In one of the references cited above, Paul indicated that Jesus would descend **in a shout,** in the **voice of an archangel** and in the trumpet of God. It appears to me that John saw similar events. The last of seven trumpets did sound in Revelation 11:15, and he will be sounding for "days" according to Revelation 10:7. In Revelation 11:15, the Greek word for "sounded" or "trumpeted" is aoristic in tense. This means, there is no limit to duration or repetition—the trumpet sounded, it is continuing to sound, and it shall be sounding. In other words, the last of the seven trumpets will still be sounding during the events in Revelation 19 when the Lord appears. In Revelation 19:17 there was also "an angel" who "cried with a loud voice" during the time when the heavens opened, and the Lord appeared on His white horse. Is this the same voice as the voice of the archangel that Paul referred to? It seems so in comparing Scriptures with Scriptures.

Thus, Jesus being seen in the open heaven as "King of kings and Lord of lords" upon His white horse may be the same event as His "appearing ... as King of kings and Lord of lords" declared by the apostle Paul in 1 Timothy 6, which is also linked to the "appearing of His coming" to annihilate the man of sin in 2 Thessalonians 2, and also linked to His coming in the shout of the archangel and the trumpet of God. Now, lets us now look at the possible coming of the Lord **"about eight days"** (about 8,000 years from when Adam was created).

The Coming of the Lord about the Eighth Day

If the accounts of Peter, Matthew, Mark, and Luke are correct, and the Scripture cannot be broken, then Jesus can come "after six days," "about eight days." That is, **"after"** six thousand years from the first Adam, the Lord should come as previously discussed, and/or **"about"** eight thousand years from when the first Adam was created, it seems like there is also another coming of the Lord. Remember Paul sated that the coning od the Lord is related to "times (plural) and seasons (plural)." This coming appears to be related to His coming to sit upon the throne of His glory to administer the eternal judgment. Therefore, let us look at Luke's account of the transfiguration that prefigures the coming of the Lord Jesus.

*Luke 9:28-29: And ... **about eight days** after these sayings ... as he prayed, the fashion of his countenance was altered ....*

The Greek word translated "about" is the Greek word **"hosei"** which is defined as: **"as if"** according to Strong's Concordance. **"Hosei"** is a compound of two words "hos" (which how) and "ei" (if). Thus, the definition by Strong's: **"as if."** Let us now insert the definition into the text and see how it reads. "And ... **'as if'** eight days ... the fashion of his countenance was altered." Or **"'which if'** eight days ... the fashion of his countenance was altered." Or **"'how if'** eight days ... the fashion of his countenance was altered."

Thus, when Jesus was transfigured, which Peter called Jesus' "power and **coming,**" this "coming" happened **"as if"** it was the eighth day. The power and coming happened **"how"** it would be **"if"** it were the eighth day (the eighth thousand years from the first Adam). Remember, it was Jesus' power and coming on the holy mount **"which"** happened as it would be **"if"** it was the eighth day.

With that said, using Peter's thousand years-day principle, Jesus' transfiguration happened **"as if"** it was the eighth (8th) thousand year from the first Adam, according to Peter's year-day principle. His transfiguration happened **"how"** it will be **"if"** it was the eighth thousand year in God's time.

Since Solomon's temple is one of the patterns of the Church of Jesus, (the "permanent" temple that Jesus is building) then the Lord may not be finished building His temple until after the seventh (7th) year, just as Solomon took seven and a half (7 ½) years[161] to build the temple. **Note**: That the Holy of Holies built by King Solomon (20 Cubits x 20 Cubits x 20 Cubits=8,000 Cubits³ which may point to 8,000 years).

1 Kings 6:37-38, NKJ: [37]*In the fourth year the foundation of the house of the LORD was laid, in the month of Ziv.* [38]*And in the eleventh year, in the month of Bul, which is the eighth month, the house was finished in all its details and according to all its plans. So, he was **seven years** in building it.*

Solomon started building the temple in the fourth (4th)[162] year of his reign, in the second month (Ziv). He completed it in the

11th year of his reign, in the eighth month (Bul). Eleven minus four, equals seven (11 - 4=7), plus six months after the month he started. Solomon started in the second month ("Ziv"); and he finished building in the eighth month ("Bul").

Thus, it took seven years and six months to build his temple; except, the temple that Jesus is building is the temple of our bodies. And Jesus' temple may also not be completed until just after seven and a half (7 ½) millennium, like Solomon's temple took 7 ½ years.

The construction of Solomon's temple ran over towards the eighth (8th) year; and the Lord's glory filled Solomon's temple with a "cloud" **after** the temple was finished.[163] The same thing is to happen after the Lord finishes building His temple. His temple will be for **"a habitation of God through the Spirit."**

*Ephesians 2:19-22, NKJ: [19]Now, therefore, you are no longer strangers and foreigners, but fellow citizens with the saints and members of the household of God, [20]having been built on the foundation of the apostles and prophets, Jesus Christ Himself being the chief cornerstone, [21]in whom the whole building, being joined together, grows into a **holy temple in the Lord,** [22]in whom you also are being built together for a **dwelling place of God in the Spirit.***

*2 Chronicles 5:1; 3; 13-14, NKJ: [1]So all the work that Solomon had done for the house of the LORD **was finished;** and Solomon brought in the things which his father David had dedicated: the silver and the gold and all the furnishings ....[3]Therefore all the men of Israel assembled with the king at the feast, which was in the **seventh month** .... [13]indeed it came to pass, when the trumpeters and singers were as one, to make one sound to be heard in praising and thanking the LORD, and when they lifted up their voice with the trumpets and cymbals and instruments of music, and praised the LORD, saying: "For He is good, For His mercy endures forever," that the house, **the house of the LORD, was filled with a cloud,***

*¹⁴so that the priests could not continue ministering because of the cloud; for the **glory of the LORD filled the house of God.***

We must also understand that as the boards of the tabernacle built by Moses continued into the Holy of Holies, the Church will also continue in the millennium. The boards are symbolic of the Body of Christ. The Holy of Holies is symbolic of the millennium rule of the resurrected saints with Christ. The "boards" of the tabernacle of Moses not only encompass the Church age (the Holy Place of 2,000 cubits); but they also made up the millennium age (the Holy of Holies of 1,000 cubits).

So, the Church will continue to be built and purged during the millennium after which God will inhabit His Church through the Spirit permanently. In other words, just because the first resurrection occurred, it does not mean that the Church will not continue[164] in the millennium to also included being purged through Jesus.

Once all the building is completed and furnished properly, on or about the eighth millennium, God will dwell in them, and they shall be His people. Therefore, it follows that as Solomon built the temple in seven (7) years, so the temple of God will be completed during the seventh millennium, prepared for the Lord to come, and inhabit His Church by His Spirit. All influence of the three beasts will be purged from humanity.

Believe it, or not, the number of the beast won't be fully purged from some people for another thousand years before God inhabits His Church by His Spirit in **fullness**. It **can** take until the eighth month (eight thousand seasons) to fully purge the influences of the number of the beast that have tainted parts of God's building.

In 1 Kings 6:37-38 we learn that Solomon finished the temple in the eighth month, seven years after the foundation was laid. Prophetically speaking, a thousand years can be divided into twelve months (1,000 years/12months=83.33 years/month). Therefore, if we multiply the eight (8) month by eighty-three, point three (83.3), it yields 666.66 (83.3 x 8 months=666.66), the number because of the beast. If we also look up the definition of the Hebrew word used for "eight," the Strong's Concordance Dictionary associates it with "anointing" (Strong's OT #8066, #8083, #8081, #8082, and # 8080).

Putting all these facts together, we can deduce that the "anointing" (in the 8th month) will purge the influence of the beast system (666.66) from the temple, which will be completed in the 7th year. This is not a strange concept, and it is nothing to be spooked about. Solomon's natural temple was influenced by the number of the beast (1 Kings 10:14; 2 Chronicles 9:13; Revelation 13:17-18).

1 Kings 10:14, NKJ: The weight of gold that came to Solomon yearly was six hundred and sixty-six talents of gold.

Revelation 13:18, NKJ: Here is wisdom. Let him who has understanding calculate the number of the beast, for it is the number of a man: His number is 666.

Luke 13:16, NKJ: "So ought not this woman, being a daughter of Abraham, whom Satan has bound -- think of it -- for eighteen years, be loosed from this bond on the Sabbath?"

Jesus loosed a woman on the Sabbath that was bound 18 years (6+6+6) by Satan—a spirit of infirmity. So likewise, on the Sabbath Day (which can be prophetic of the Sabbath Millennium) the "woman" (the continuing Church) who was bound for 18 years (6+6+6) will be loosed from Satan and the beast influence (Luke 13:16, Revelation 20:1-3). Jesus will be freeing humanity from the influence of Satan by binding the

Devil in the abyss and casting the other two beasts into the lake of fire.

*Revelation 19:20: And **the beast was taken,** and with him **the false prophet** that wrought miracles before him, with which he deceived them that had received the mark of the beast, and them that worshipped his image. **These both were cast alive into a lake of fire** burning with brimstone.*

*Revelation 20:1-3: [1]And I saw an angel come down from heaven, having the key of the bottomless pit and a great chain in his hand. [2]And he laid hold on the dragon, that old serpent, which is the Devil, and Satan, and **bound him a thousand years**, [3]And cast him into the bottomless pit, and shut him up, and set a seal upon him, **that he should deceive the nations no more…***

The Scripture also teaches through the molten sea that Solomon built, its dimensions and its design, that the "washing" of the "priest" (that was started by John Wycliffe's[165] reformation) from the effect of the beast system will not be fully realized in "conquest" unless the sea is filled up to three thousand baths.

*1 Kings 7:23-26: [23]And he made a **molten sea,** ten cubits from the one brim to the other: it was round all about, and his height was five cubits: and a line of thirty cubits did compass it round about …. [26]And it was a hand breadth thick, and the brim thereof was wrought like the brim of a cup, with flowers of lilies: it contained **two thousand baths.***

*2 Chronicles 4:2-6: [2]Also he made a molten sea of ten cubits from brim to brim, round in compass, and five cubits the height thereof; and a line of thirty cubits did compass it round about …. [5]And the thickness of it was a handbreadth, and the brim of it like the work of the brim of a cup, with flowers of lilies; and it **received and held three thousand baths.** [6]… but the sea was for the **priests to wash in.***

*Revelation 15:2, NAU: And I saw something like a sea of glass mixed with fire, and those who had been **victorious over** (lit., out of) the **beast** and his **image** and the **number of his name,** standing on the sea of glass, holding harps of God.*

This molten Sea is a direct correlation to the sea of glass mingled with fire that was used to purge those who were victorious out of the beast, out of its image, and out of the number of its name in Revelation 15. "Molten" is also translated as "harden" in Job 38:38. The sea of glass is a "hard sea." "Molten" also has to do with cast metal, hence its association with heat or fire. The sea of glass is mingled with fire. This is baptism or a washing in fire on a sea of glass.

The molten sea is usually filled with two thousand baths; however, it can receive and hold three thousand baths. These baths correspond to the distance from Jesus' first coming until the three thousand years after His first coming is completed. The molten sea was also used for the washing of the **priests.** This means that the "those" in Revelation 15:2 were people who were a part of the beast system, but they received Jesus' "righteousness" and were being purged from their former defilement, since they are effectively a part of his holy nation and royal priesthood. Remember all believers are justified by Jesus' righteous acts, only.

*Romans 5:18, NKJ: Therefore, as through one man's offense judgment came to all men, resulting in condemnation, even so **through one Man's righteous act** the free gift came to all men, resulting in **justification of life.***

*Revelation 15:4, YLT: Who may not fear Thee, O Lord, and glorify Thy name? Because Thou alone art kind, because all the nations shall come and bow before Thee, because Thy **righteous acts** were manifested.*

The priests on the sea of glass mingled with fire were victorious "out of" the beast's influences because of the "manifestation of [Jesus'] righteous acts" that they referenced in the song of the Lamb. "Who may not fear Thee, O Lord, and glorify Thy name? Because Thou alone art kind, because all the nations shall come and bow before Thee, because Thy **righteous acts** were manifested" (Revelation 15:4, YLT). Yes, they received salvation, not by being down down-judged, but by the manifestation of the Lord's righteous acts![166]

Here is an interpretation of what I just wrote, the three thousand (3,000) baths can point to the three thousand (3,000) years from the last Adam, Jesus, to the time that it will take to wash away the influence of the beast nature. Three thousand years from the last Adam is the same end if one counts seven thousand years from the first Adam. It is also important to note that it was on the sea of glass that it was said that they had the "**victory**" out of the beast.

This is because the author of 2 Chronicles indicated that the molten sea "received and held" three thousand baths. "Received and held three thousand baths" can also literally reads, "**conquered** and maintained three thousand baths." Again, this can be interpreted to show that it will take all three thousand years from Christ to "**victoriously**" purge or "**conquer**" the influence of the beast system out of some believer; yet it can take even until the eighth millennium, which is the same as saying it may take up to the end of seven thousand years from the first Adam, or to the end of three thousand years from the last, Adam—Jesus.

Even though the beast and the false prophet were cast into the lake of fire just before the beginning of the seventh millennium, their influence will be washed away with fire. God is still delivering man from the beastly nature, including delivering mankind from being subject to death, like beasts.[167]

At the end of the seventh millennium, Death and Hell will be completely vanquished

When Jesus Comes to Sit on the Throne of His Glory

Matthew 25:31-32; 41, NKJ: [31]*"When the Son of Man comes in His glory, and all the holy angels with Him, then He will sit on the throne of His glory.* [32]*"All the nations will be gathered before Him, and He will separate them* ...[41]*"Then He will also say to those on the left hand, 'Depart from Me ... into the **everlasting fire** prepared for the devil and his angels....'"*

Another reason it appears that Jesus will also **come after** the seventh millennium is outlined in Jesus' teaching in Matthew 25:31-46. Jesus does say that "the Son of man [Jesus] will **come** in His glory and all the holy angels with Him." The same discourse given by Jesus also states that after His coming, Jesus will sit on the throne of His glory to issue eternal judgments.

It is <u>after</u> His coming in His glory to sit upon the throne of His glory that Jesus commands **some** to "**depart ... into the everlasting fire prepared for the devil and his angels.**" According to Revelation 20:10-15, the devil and **those who are not found written in the Book** of Life are cast into the lake of fire and lightning-brimstone **after** the millennium rule of Christ with the saints of first resurrection is completed.

Thus, according to Matthew (Matthew 25:31-46) and John (Revelation 20:7-15), it appears that Jesus will also come in glory after the seventh millennium at which time Gog and Magog is manifested; and at which time Satan and those not found written in the book of life will go to the lake of fire — the second death.

That is, just as people, some angels and Satan were not sent to the lake of fire until after[168] the millennium rule of Christ with

His resurrected saints, as described in Revelation 20:10-15, so likewise Matthew 25:31-46, indicates that the sending of some people to the lake of fire happens **after** Jesus comes in His glory to sit upon His throne. This coming appears to be **after** the end of the 7th millennium from the first Adam, which is also called the millennium rule of Christ with the first resurrection saints. That is, in Revelation 20:11, the great white throne and the eternal judgment associated with it, manifested after the seventh millennium is completed.

Thus, by way of review, the Lord will manifest in His coming at the beginning of the seventh millennium to defeat His enemies Satan, the beast and the false prophet gathered against Jesus and His armies. Jesus will cast the beast, the false prophet into the lake of fire; and He will also destroy the nations that follow the beast and the false prophet, feeding them to birds from mid-heaven, at which time the strong angel will also bind Satan; with the phases of first resurrection apparently concluding; **and** it appears that Jesus will yet come again at the beginning of the eighth millennium to send Satan to the lake of fire. He will also be sending those who are not found written in the Book of Life to the lake of fire; then Death and Hell will also go to the lake of fire.

The Resurrection of they that are Christ's at His Coming

*1 Corinthians 15:22-23: For as in Adam all die, even so in Christ shall all be made alive. 23 But every man in his **own order:** the '**firstfruit Christ;**' afterward **they that are Christ's** at his coming.*

For many years, men have developed their own doctrines concerning Christ's coming back to the earth. Some have declared a resurrection that is not necessarily Scriptural. The truth is: there is a condition associated with being "part" of the resurrection in Jesus' coming.

The only condition is that a person must be "in Christ," as we learned in a previous chapter, or a person must be "of Christ." A person must "belong to Christ," or in the words of the Scriptures above, **"they that are Christ's** at His coming."

This phrase **"they that are Christ"** or **"the ones of Christ"** is only translated as such in one other place in the Scripture as we will review in detail later in this chapter. According to Galatians 5:24, "... *they that are Christ's have crucified the flesh with the affections and lusts."*

Thus, in the strictest sense of the meaning of the phrase, the resurrection at Jesus' physical coming will include "the ones of Christ" who through the Holy Spirit have "crucified the flesh with its 'emotions' and lusts." With that said, there are also other Scriptures that broaden the field of those who are "of Christ."

"Christ's" in the statement "they that are **Christ's"** is possessive in case, which shows ownership or association. In the Greek text, the words "are Christ's" is genitive in case, which means that Christ is their source. That is, "they that are Christ's" are born **from** Christ and **belong** to Christ. Jesus owns us; because we were purchased by His blood, the blood of His cross,[169] a purchase that can only be secured by the seal of the Spirit until the redemption of the purchaser's possession (Ephesians 1:13-14).

As indicated earlier, the phrase, "they that are Christ's," literally reads "the ones **of Christ.**" Thus, the ones **"of"** Christ will be resurrected in Jesus' coming. Paul said, "The Body is **of** Christ;" and not of the law (legalistic rituals). Thus, Jesus will be resurrecting a corporate body that belongs to Him; a Body that is **of** Him, when He returns in the same way He went to heaven.

The Body is of Christ

Colossians 2:16-17: [16]*Let no man therefore judge you in meat, or in drink, or in respect of a holyday, or of the new moon, or of the Sabbath [days]:* [17]*Which are a shadow of things to come; but **the body [is] of Christ.***

When Christ comes physically and that resurrection occurs, the Body **of** Christ will be raised. A person must belong to Christ's Body to be raised in His coming, as opposed to belonging to a legalistic body. Legalism can mean excessive rules of "do's and don'ts."

Legalism can be defined as a person trying to attain justification by works, rather than by the faith of Christ.[170] During His coming, the Lord may not raise from the dead any legalistic body of so-called believers. The Body is of Christ. Thus, the Body is not of legalism.

Colossians 2:16-17: [16]*Let no man therefore judge you in meat, or in drink, or in respect of a holyday, or of the new moon, or of the Sabbath [days]:* [17]*Which are a **shadow** of things to come; but **the body [is] of Christ.***

Page | 104

Paul indicated that the Body of Christ is not a legalistic body being judged by what a person, eats, and drinks (ceremonially or otherwise), observing holydays, etc. When a religion stresses legalism concerning eating certain meat, that legalistic body of so-called believers is considered a "shadow" and "weak."[171]

The Bible said all meats are to be received by us, when the meats are sanctified by prayer.[172] Legalism is also at work through those who are condemning saints or people who drink.[173] Paul said, "Let no man therefore judge you ... in drink." The Bible said drunkenness is forbidden, not drinking. The disciples drank real wine in the days of Paul. The problem was that they abused drinking. They abused drinking by getting drunk with the communion wine in; and Paul indicated that if they wanted to drink it should have done at home.[174]

Yet, a person should not prophesy wine and strong drink.[175] Believers must also be very considerate of those whose "consciences" are "weak" towards certain days, foods, and drinks.[176] However, we must not condemn people to hell for drinking.[177]

Legalists also emphasize so called "holy days" or "feasts." Even present-day religions that emphasize "no work" on their Sabbath are legalistic.[178] Listen to what the apostle Paul said to the Galatians: "You observe days, and months, and times, and years. **I am afraid of you,** lest I have bestowed upon you labor in **vain.**"[179]

These are the legalistic works that make a body of so-called believers not of Christ, **observing days, and months, and times, and years.** We are supposed to be "afraid" of people like that. Paul was afraid of legalists! Why? Legalism makes apostolic labor, **"vain."** Legalism also disqualifies a person from partaking of grace![180] Remember, the Body is **of** Christ. Christ's Body is <u>not</u> supposed to be legalistic!

Observing years means people who legalistically have yearly events, like pastors' yearly anniversary, etc. Where in the Bible does it say we are to have pastors' anniversary every year? **Observing times** exposes the popular concept of "revival times," zodiac observation, etc.; **months** points to excessively observing worldly seasonal events in the Church of Jesus (i.e., Easter, Valentine's Day, and so on).

Finally, **"observing days"** points to the religiosity of men's day, women's day, choir day, horoscopes, etc. Legalism is also linked to <u>over</u> emphasizing certain kinds of dress codes for preachers and saints. I do not have to wear a collar to show that I am a preacher. I am already dressed with glory and beauty in the Spirit by the greater Aaron (Jesus).

The truth is, Peter and Paul did say that we are to dress moderately, with an emphasis on dressing with a meek and quiet spirit. Yet, dressing in moderation is not supposed to become legalistic (the leaders telling people "what" to wear). Predetermined seating, excessively long public prayer, and so on are also legalistic and religious (outward ceremonies).[181]

Paul also said the legalist things of the law of Judaism are "a **shadow** of things to come." The writer of Hebrews indicated the same: "For the **law having a shadow** of good things to come, [and] not the very image of the things...."[182] Those "things to come" have come. Jesus, the Christ, and His Clean Spirit are come in the flesh.[183] The Body is now of Christ.

The body is not of the law that works death. The Body has always been of Christ. The Holy Spirit who baptizes us into the Body of Christ works life and peace. Thus, they that are Christ's, those who belong to the "Body of Christ," (those who are not given to legalism, but those who are baptized into one Body by the Holy Spirit) will be resurrected in His coming.[184]

We will be resurrected because we have faith in His blood that we are indeed "blood bought."[185] "It is **not of works** least any man should boast!"[186] Jesus' blood is strong enough!

They That Are Christ's Are Purchased with Jesus' Blood

*Acts 20:28: Take heed therefore unto yourselves, and to all the flock, over the which the Holy Ghost hath made you overseers, to feed the church of God, **which he hath purchased with his own blood.***

*1Corinthains 6:20: **For you are bought with a price:** therefore, glorify God in your body, and in your spirit, **which are God's.***

If a person goes to a store to buy an item and pay for an item fully, that item belongs to the purchaser. God has purchased His Church through the blood of Jesus. The price that God paid for us was the price of His own blood. The Scriptures above say, **"For you are bought with a price," "purchased with His own blood."**

Thus, whosoever believes that Jesus is the Christ, the Son of God, is born of God.[187] Thus, Jesus is our "propitiatory shelter through faith in His blood."[188] Jesus is also our **"mercy seat through faith in His blood."**[189]

Jesus is our Buyer who now owns us. We who believe in His blood belong to Jesus. There is a salvation that is purchased for us through the Lord Jesus Christ that is linked to living in the resurrection with Jesus.

*1 Thessalonians 5:9-10: [9]For God hath not appointed us to wrath, **but to obtain salvation by our Lord Jesus Christ,** [10]Who died for us, that, whether we wake or sleep, **we should live together with him.***

"But to obtain salvation …." is literally translated as **"but into the purchased salvation** through our Lord Jesus Christ." Jesus purchased salvation for us that "we should **live together with Him**." He purchased this through His own blood. We belong to Him through faith in His blood. We are that treasure or that pearl in the field that Jesus bought when He purchased the entire field.[190] Jesus' blood is one of the witnesses to us that we indeed belong to Christ in His coming.

"There are three that bear record … the Spirit, and the water, and **the blood**."[191] Therefore, those who believe in the blood of Jesus have been purchased by the same blood. Paul declared that because we are bought with the price of blood, our bodies, and spirits **"are God's."**

*1 Corinthians 6:20: For you are **bought with a price:** therefore, glorify God in your **body,** and in your **spirit, which are God's.***

*1 Corinthians 6:19, N: Or do you not know that your body is the temple of the Holy Spirit who is in you, whom you have from God, and **you are not your own?***

Our bodies and spirits "which are God's" is now "the temple of the Holy 'Spirit' … and you are not your own." Because we are not our own, Jesus owns us. It follows that in the coming of our Lord Jesus, those bodies that are purchased by Jesus' blood will be resurrected by Jesus.

We are no longer our own, our bodies now belong to the Spirit of God. Thus, we must glorify Him in our bodies and spirits. We must allow the Holy Spirit to crucify the residue of the flesh nature in our bodies. This is important because, those who belong to Jesus Christ have crucified the flesh.

This may be sobering for some to know. However, only "they that are Christ's" will experience resurrection at His coming. This means that we, who are in Christ Jesus, must <u>also</u> allow our flesh to be crucified. "For... **in Christ** shall all be made alive... **they that are Christ's ....**"

They That Are Christ's Have Crucified the Flesh

*Galatians 5:24: And **they that are Christ's** have **crucified the flesh** with the affections (lit., sufferings, or emotions) and lusts.*

Galatians 5:24 cited above provides a definition for "they that are Christ's." Paul said, "They that are Christ's **have crucified the flesh** with its **'sufferings'** and **lust.**" So, we show that we belong to Christ if we also crucify the "emotions" of the flesh nature and lust. How do we crucify emotional lust and the emotional flesh nature?

First, the answer is Jesus already crucified the old nature for us. This is good news! Our old man (man of sin) was crucified with Jesus and the Scripture says that this is something we should **"know." "Knowing** this, that **our old man** is crucified with him, that the **body of sin** might be destroyed, that henceforth we should not serve sin."[192]

We are to **"know"** that "the old man," another name for the **"man of sin,"** is indeed crucified with Jesus. Paul also stated something similar in Galatians 2:20. Paul stated that **"I am crucified with Christ** ...and the life which I now live in the flesh **I live by the faith of the Son of God**, who loved me, and gave himself for me." We really need to **"know"** this.

Our sin nature is crucified. Jesus' crucifixion was a gift to us. "He **gave** Himself for us." We are to receive His gift to us. Sins were ended, and transgressions were finished through the cross of Christ, according to Daniel 9. We do not have to live like that old man of sin anymore because of Jesus' gift to us.

Secondly, "crucified" in Galatians 5:24, is in the **"active voice"** and **"aorist tense"** in the Greek text. Active voice means that the subject participates in the action. Aorist tense means an action that occurred in the past with ongoing results not referencing time, duration, and repetition. The subject of Galatians 5:24 is **"they that are Christ's."**

Thus, they that are Christ's are to participate in the action of crucifying the flesh with its lust and emotions daily. Jesus also said that his "disciple" must participate in taking up their own cross. Jesus said it this way: "If any man will come after me, let him **deny (lit., contradict)** himself, and **take up his cross, and follow me."** [193]

Thus, the list of the "works of the flesh" [194] Paul later referred to in Galatians 5:24 **"were crucified"** by Jesus. Now we must also crucify the works of the flesh experientially through Jesus' Spirit. We must not allow these fleshly works to contradict the work of Jesus' cross by allowing **"lust against the Spirit."** [195] We, on the other hand, must **"contradict"** the lusts of the flesh by reckoning them crucified. We do this by walking in the Spirit or "minding the Spirit." [196]

Strongholds of fleshly (or disobedient) thoughts that exalt themselves against the knowledge of God are demolished with force through the Spirit of God. [197] Thus any lust that attempts to exalt itself against the truth that the lust of the flesh **has indeed been crucified** must be demolished through the ability of the Holy Spirit.

The Scripture states that when we "walk in the Spirit" we "shall not **fulfill (lit., complete)** the lust of the flesh." [198] In other words, the flesh does indeed cause "lust against the Spirit;" however, we through the Spirit of Christ must not allow lust to **"complete"** its longings, or "on-feelings." The lust of the flesh ("the body of sin") must be "contradicted" and mortified by the leading of the Holy Spirit. [199] This crucifixion (contradiction) of fleshly desires through the Spirit is a witness to us that we are indeed Christ's.

Saying it another way, we are the sons of God when we allow the Spirit of God to lead us to put to death any sinful **"practices"** of the Body. "For if you live after the flesh, you shall die: but if you through the Spirit do mortify the deeds of the body, you shall live. **For** as many as are **led** by the Spirit of God, they are the sons of God."[200]

The conjunction **"for"** at the beginning of the sentence in verse 14, tells us that allowing the "leading" of the Spirit to mortify the deeds of the body is what makes us the sons of God. We are Christ's because we have crucified the flesh by His Spirit, and **we do not "complete"** lustful conceptions against the Spirit.

Saints must be watchful to ensure that no lust seizes or clasps them, which then births sin, and then breeds death.[201] With that said, I must add grace here by saying that the Scripture allows mercy for "short comings" by saying that "if any man sin we have an advocate with the Father, Jesus, the righteous."[202]

If we say that we have no sin, we deceive ourselves, and the truth is not in us. If we confess our sins, he is faithful and just to forgive us [our] sins, and to cleanse us from all unrighteousness.[203]

Finally, the **"affections** of the flesh,"** which literally reads, **"sufferings** of the flesh," or **"emotions** of the flesh" are also to be crucified according to Paul. **"They that are Christ's have crucified ... the affections (sufferings, emotions) and lusts."**

The Greek word for **"affections"** or **"sufferings"** is also translated as **"inordinate affections"** in Colossians 3:5. Paul also coupled these words (lust and affections) again when he referred to "sexual immorality" or "fornication" in 1 Thessalonians 4:3-5.

In 1 Thessalonians 4, Paul calls fornication the **"lust of concupiscence"** which literally reads the **"suffering of lusts,"** or **"the emotions of on-feelings."** Therefore, there are some lusts (feelings on the flesh) that may cause a believer to "suffer" "emotionally" for no good reason. As indicated earlier, Paul listed one of these lusts that caused bad emotions as "fornication" or "sexual immorality" relative to men **"overreaching"** sexually towards other men and/or women.

The Thessalonians were encouraged to learn how to **"possess"** their "vessels in sanctification and honor."[204] Apparently there was some uncalled for "emotional suffering" among some in that Church related to sexual "lust," or sexual "on-feelings." This same idea is also conveyed to the Romans in Romans 1:26-27 concerning "men 'in' men" and women with women.

Romans 1:26-27: *[26]For this cause, God gave them up unto **vile affections (lit., dishonored sufferings, or dishonoring emotions):** for even their women did change the natural use into that which is against nature: [27]And likewise also the men, leaving the natural use of the woman, burned in their lust one toward another; **men with men** working that which is unseemly, and receiving in themselves that recompense of their error which was meet.*

In the verse above **"dishonored sufferings" or "dishonoring emotions"** are used relative to women who "changed their natural use into that which is against nature," women with women; and the phrase is also used concerning men who sent away the natural use of the women, which Paul called **"men 'in' men."** Paul classified these practices as the type of "emotional suffering" which has **no value** or **no honor.**

By the way, one of the emotional sufferings that this type of lust produces is the emotion that diminishes the estimation of one's self-worth (low self-esteem). That is, some of the participants of this type of sexual immorality suffer emotionally by feeling devalued, disfigured, or deformed. Some may even deny these facts publicly, but in their secret chambers upon their beds, their thoughts are different; and more importantly, the Scriptures that declare these byproducts of sexual immorality are infallible.

These are a few of the fleshly emotional suffering which devalue the body. Yet, a Believer must see these emotional sufferings as crucified through Christ and that these sufferings of the flesh must remain mortified through the Spirit of life in Christ Jesus.

This "law of the Spirit of Life in Christ Jesus" is a key to being sustained as "free" sons of God. We are sealed **"in"** Him.[205] As long as His "Anointing" of the Holy Spirit remains in us, and if we are not "seduced" to wander from His loving care, we are destined to be raised from the dead by Jesus.[206]

We are Christ's, because the flesh with its lusts and emotions are crucified through the crucifixion of Jesus. We are Christ's if we continue to crucify ("contradict") the flesh and do not "complete" any temptations of the flesh.

Jesus has sent forth the Spirit of Adoption into hearts crying Abba, Father. The Holy Spirit is there to encourage us to continue to mortify any sinful deeds of the body. The fact that we now have His Holy Spirit living in us also witnesses to us that we belong to Christ.

*Romans 8:9: But you are not in the flesh, but in the Spirit, **if so be that**[207] the **Spirit of God** dwell in you. **Now if any man has not the Spirit of Christ, he is none of his.***

Before, I continue, let me make a clarification concerning the Holy Spirit. Some have tried to separate the "Spirit of Christ" from the "Spirit of Jesus." However, the Scriptures state that "God has made ...Jesus...**both** Lord and Christ."[208] Thus, the "Spirit of Christ" is the "Spirit of Jesus" is "the Spirit of the Lord."

The Spirit of Christ is "the Spirit of the Lord;" and all these names are synonymous with the Spirit of God or the Holy Spirit. We should not complicate things because Romans 8:11; 8:13 and 8:14 also described the Spirit of Christ as the "Spirit of God" that raised Jesus from the dead.

With that said, we can see that **"having the Spirit of Christ"** is the Spirit who makes us "belong" to Christ. This is true because the Scripture states that if we do not have Christ's Spirit we do not belong to Jesus, "Now if any man **have not** the Spirit of Christ, he is **none of His.**" Thus, if we **do have** His Spirit, we **do** belong to Christ, Jesus; and the Holy Spirit that we received from God is a gift.[209]

*Acts 2:38-39: [38]Then Peter said unto them, **Repent,** and be baptized every one of you in the name of Jesus Christ for the remission of sins, and you shall receive the **gift** of the Holy Ghost. [39]For the promise is unto **you,** and to **your children,** and to **all that are afar off,** even **as many** as the Lord our God shall call.*

It must be understood that the Holy Spirit is a gift for **"all,"** including us who **"are afar off"** from the time that the Spirit was first poured out into the first one hundred and twenty disciples of Jesus. The Holy Spirit is a gift; thus, there should be no divisive boasting of one against another.

That is, none of us should say "I belong to Christ because I have the Holy Spirit and you do not."[210] Brothers and sisters, let us not boast as if the Holy Spirit we have received is not a gift.[211] Why? God's **"ownership"** of us (His Saints) <u>begins</u> with the blood of Jesus and is then guaranteed by the seal of His Spirit.

*Acts 20:28: Take heed therefore unto yourselves, and to all the flock, over the which the Holy Ghost hath made you overseers, to feed the church of God, which **he hath purchased with his own blood.***

*1 Corinthians 6:20: For you are **bought with a price**: therefore, glorify God in your body, and in your spirit, which are God's.*

Ephesians 1:13-14, NKJ: [13]*In Him you also trusted, after you heard the word of truth, the gospel of your salvation; in whom also, having believed, **you were sealed with the Holy Spirit** of promise,* [14]*who is the **guarantee** of our inheritance **until the redemption of the purchased possession,** to the praise of His glory.*

The references above explicitly indicate that we are purchased by the blood of Jesus. Thus, God's ownership of us starts when we apply the blood of Jesus to our hearts. In addition, there are three that bear record; the water (water baptism), blood (Jesus' blood which looses sin(s)), and the Holy Spirit (who is the Truth and who bears witness in us that we indeed belong to Christ).[212]

Along with blood and water or water and blood, Jesus also gives us a personal down payment or pledge that guarantees His ownership of us. This guarantee is the gift of the Holy Spirit.[213] And according to Paul, if we do not have ("hold") the Spirit of Christ we are none of His. Listen to the Amplified Bible.

Romans 8:9, AMP: But you are not living the life of the flesh, you are living the life of the Spirit, if the [Holy] Spirit of God [really] dwells within you [directs and controls you]. **But if anyone does not possess the [Holy] Spirit of Christ, he is none of His [he does not belong to Christ, is not truly a child of God].** *[Romans 8:14.]*

The next questions are: At what point do believers receive the Spirit of Christ? How does a Believer know that they have received this gift? If a person does not have the Holy Spirit, do they miss the first resurrection? **The Scriptures indicate that receiving the Holy Spirit is a separate experience from being born of the Spirit;** and the infilling of the Spirit in us can <u>reoccur</u>, as God wills.

In Acts 2:4, there is no doubt that the disciples received the Holy Spirit as a unique experience, because they believed in Jesus. "They were all filled with the Holy Ghost, and **began to speak with other tongues,** as the Spirit gave them utterance." Yet these same disciples were **filled again** in Acts 4:31 after Peter led a prayer meeting. "And when they had prayed, the place was shaken where they were assembled together; and they were **all filled with the Holy Ghost, and** they spoke the word of God with boldness."

The Same thing happened to Paul, he was filled with the Holy Spirit in Acts 9:17 and was **filled again** in Acts 13:9. With that said, being filled with the Holy Spirit is a unique experience in the three phases of salvation. Cornelius, a Gentile, and his household also received the Holy Spirit in a unique experience after they believed Peter's preaching concerning Jesus.

Acts 10:44-46: *44While Peter yet spoke these words,* **the Holy Ghost fell on** *all them which heard the word.* *45And they of the circumcision which believed were astonished, as many as came with Peter, because that on the Gentiles also was poured out the* **gift of the Holy Ghost.** *46For they heard them speak with tongues, and* *magnify God, then answered Peter,* ⁴⁷*Can any man forbid water, that these should not be baptized, which have* **received** *the Holy Ghost as well as we?*

There can be no doubt that a unique event happened to Cornelius and his household. They "received the Holy Spirit" **as** Peter and the rest of the Jewish believers have in Acts 2, and so on. The experience at Cornelius' home was heard by Peter and his six companions. "They **heard** them **speak with tongues and magnify God.**" A similar thing happened to a <u>whole</u> Church at Ephesus.

"After they believed," they also were "sealed with the Holy Spirit" the "earnest" (lit., guarantee, or pledge) of their inheritance.[214] When did the Church of Ephesus receive the Spirit as a guarantee? The answer is: **"After** they believed;" and how did they know that they received the Spirit? They also both spoke in tongues and prophesied!

Acts 19:1-2; 6: ¹*And it came to pass ..., Paul having passed through the upper coasts came to Ephesus: and finding certain disciples,* ²*He said unto them, have you* **received the** *Holy Ghost* **since you believed?** *And they said unto him, we have not so much as heard whether there be any Holy Ghost...*⁶*And when Paul had laid his hands upon them,* **the Holy Ghost came on them;** *and* **they spoke with tongues and prophesied.**

This text documented how the Church at Ephesus received the Holy Spirit. They were "sealed" with "the guarantee of their inheritance" **<u>after</u>** they believed, and after Paul laid hands on them.

And as I asked earlier, how did Paul and the Church of Ephesus know that they were filled? They heard words! In this case, Paul heard **both**[215] words of tongues **and** words of prophecy. The last part of verse six literally reads: "...the Holy Spirit came on them and they spoke **'both'** with tongues and prophesied." In Peter's case at Cornelius' house, Peter also heard words of tongues **and** words that "magnified God."

The foremost sign of being filled with the Holy Spirit appears to be "word" or "words" being heard. These spoken words also appear to be primarily in tongues. However, these words appear to be not just words of unknown tongues, even though speaking in a tongue is a prevalent indication of being filled with the Holy Spirit.

These words can be a strong utterance of "magnifying God," and "prophesying." Again, it appears that the evidence of receiving the Holy Spirit is indeed primarily with "words" been spoken by the recipients. The Church of Ephesus spoke **both** tongues and prophecy.

However, each person may differ in what "kind" of words or differ in what kind of "dialect"[216] they may speak after receiving the Holy Spirit. It must also be understood that a Spirit filled life may also manifest without words, we call this the "fruit of the Spirit," which deals more with the growth of the "character" of Christ in them. Believers need both the fruit and the gifts manifesting in their lives.

The Scripture teaches that there are diversities of the gifts of the Spirit, but it is the same Spirit who manifests these diversities; there are diversities of administering these gifts, but the same Lord; and there are diversities of operations but the same God. The Scriptures did not stop there. Paul also stated that there are <u>different</u> **"manifestations of the Spirit,"** meaning, the evidence of the Spirit filled life **"manifests"** in various ways.

*1 Corinthians 12:7-11: [7]But **the manifestation** of the Spirit is given to every man to profit withal. [8]For to one is given by the Spirit the **word of wisdom**; to **another the word of knowledge** by the same Spirit; [9]To **another faith** by the same Spirit; to **another the***

Page | 118

gifts of healing by the same Spirit; [10]*To another the working of miracles; to another prophecy; to another discerning of spirits; to another divers kinds of tongues; to another the interpretation of tongues:* [11]*But all these works that one and the selfsame Spirit, dividing to every man severally as he will.*

"**The manifestation** (singular) of the Spirit" differs. As seen above, the Spirit manifest Himself in at least nine different ways; yet the Bible calls these nine gifts a "manifestation (singular)." There are indeed "the manifestation" of "species of tongues" or "species of dialects,"[217] "the manifestation" of prophecy,[218] "the manifestation" of words of magnifying God (declaring Jesus is Lord),[219] "the manifestation" of "word (lit., logos) of wisdom," "the manifestation" of "word (lit., logos) of knowledge,"[220] the manifestation of the Spirit of faith that speaks,[221] and so on.

What about the manifestation of a Spirit filled life in the "fruit of the Spirit:" love, joy, peace, faith, longsuffering, gentleness, meekness, kindness, temperance, righteousness, and so on?[222] Please note that if one speaks in tongues <u>without having love</u> (a fruit of the Spirit), speaking in tongues is nothing more than an "'echoing' brass, or a 'screaming' symbol."[223] Thus, being filled with the "fruit of love" is profitable.

I am not convinced that "all" will speak in tongues when they are filled. What if some when they are filled **"cry"** "Abba, Father" after being filled?[224] What if some only manifest that they are filled with the Holy Spirit by the miracles they perform by the Spirit; or what if some have a strong ability to discern spirits (God's, humans,' angels,' demons,' the false prophet's, etc.)? The **manifestation** of the Holy Spirit is by **nine** "differences of administrations, but the same Lord."[225] The fruit of the Holy Spirit is seen in nine ways, but remains singular, "fruit (singular) of the Spirit."[226]

It is also possible to be filled with the Holy Spirit in the womb where the baby cannot speak words.[227] Elizabeth knew John was filled in her womb, because the baby leaped in her womb. She had the witness in herself. **"It is the Spirit that bears witness, because the Spirit is truth."**[228] **"The Spirit itself bears witness with our spirit, that we are the children of God."**[229]

This is how one knows that they are Christ's; the Spirit will bear witness with our spirits that we are indeed the "offspring" of God. If you have the Spirit of the Son in you, you will eventually cry, "Abba Father." There should be a leaping or a witness in your spiritual womb when you are filled with the Christ.

Who can explain a baby being filled in the womb? Who can "say to [God], what have you done?" The "I Am" is sovereign. The Almighty can do what He wants to do whenever He wants to do it, and who can limit Him? We cannot find out His "decision," they are "inscrutable!"[230] His "ways are "untraceable!"[231]

How many people have their faith overthrown by incomplete doctrines, by people saying unless a person speaks with tongues **right away** that person is not filled? **It is the Spirit that bears witness, not man!** The Holy Spirit "manifests" Himself to each person as it **profits God,** and as it profits each person. It may not profit God for some to speak in tongues, immediately, and then it may profit God for some to speak in tongues of angels.[232]

Thus, the question to us is: will all speak with tongues? As we will see through the Scriptures in a moment, I believe the apparent answer is **no!** Now note, I did not say "can" all speak in tongues, which speaks of the "possibility" of all speaking. The answer would be yes, "all things are 'possible' through

God." The question is does it profit God for all to speak in tongues? Is speaking in a tongue greater than prophecy?[233] Did God make the entire body a tongue?

1 Corinthians 12:29-30: [29]*Are all apostles? Are all prophets? Are all teachers? Are all workers of miracles?* [30]*Have all the gifts of healing?* ***Do all speak with tongues?*** *Do all interpret?*

The Greek texts (Received text, Byzantine text, and Alexandrian text) for the verses above read as such: [29]*Not all apostles. Not all prophets. Not all teachers. Not all powers.* [30] *Not all hold the graces of healing.* ***Not all are speaking tongues.*** *Not all are interpreting.*

First, one should note that Paul gave a qualifying statement indicating that **"not all"** function in all the gifts. With respect to my topic for this section, Paul stated that **"Not all are speaking tongues."** Paul's statement as seen in the Greek texts[234] is clear.

All will not speak in tongues. With that said, if we look at the English translation concerning the question, do all speak in tongues? Paul asked a series of questions in 1 Corinthians 12:29-30, whose answers are obviously **no.**

"Are all apostles?" **The answer is no!** Everyone in the Body of Christ is not an apostle! "Are all prophets?" **Again, the answer is obviously no** (even though today there are many self-appointed (false) prophets)! "Are all teachers?" **No!**

"Are all workers of miracles?" **No!** "Have all the **gifts (plural)** of healing?" **No again!** Some are gifted to heal broken hearts like Jesus, and others are gifted to perform physical healing like Jesus.

Here is the big question, "do all speak with tongues?" Gathering from the rest of the apparent answers to Paul's questions, the answer to this question is also no; and **remember,** the Greek text **explicitly says,** **"Not all** are speaking tongues" (see also NAU).

Finally, "Do all interpret?" The answer is no! Paul indicated in 1 Corinthians 14 that if no interpreter of tongues is present in a Church meeting, then those who speak in tongues are to speak to themselves or pray that they may interpret themselves. Gathering from Paul's directive to the Corinthians, everyone does not interpret tongues, either!

With all the above in mind, it would really look deformed if the whole body were a big fat tongue lying in the Church building; because, per the original texts, **"Not all are speaking tongues!"** What if the whole body was a big toe sitting in the Church building? The human body has many parts. The whole human body is not a big tongue. I urge the reader to read 1 Corinthians 12 again, the entire chapter, and read it slowly for correct understanding.

Thus, all may not necessarily speak in tongues when they receive the Holy Spirit, but I believe "a word" or "words" will be spoken through the Spirit to substantiate that unique experience; and/or some kind of cry to the Father that shows the Holy Spirit has indeed filled that person.[235]

Note: I do believe that there are believers who speak in tongues after being filled with the Holy Spirit; and potentially, all those who "believe" (have the faith) to speak in tongues, will.[236] Yet, everyone may not speak with tongues as we saw in Paul's writing above, and yet they are filled with the Holy Spirit.

The manifestation of the Holy Spirit is seen in at least nine ways; and speaking in tongues are only one of the ways the Spirit manifests. Some may "cry, Abba, Father."[237] Some may magnify God as Cornelius' household did. For one to say Jesus is Lord (which is the same as "magnifying" Jesus), they must have the Spirit.[238]

There are other witnesses of spoken words associated with being filled with the Spirit of Christ.[239] This is true in Luke's record of the Samaritan Believers receiving the Spirit. "Word" was heard, but what word? When the apostles laid hands on the new converts in Samaria, they also spoke **"logos (lit., word, or exposed thought)."**

Acts 8:14-21: [14]*Now when the apostles which were at Jerusalem heard that Samaria had received the word of God, they sent unto them Peter and John:* [15]*Who, when they were come down, prayed for them,* **that they might receive the Holy Ghost** ... [17]**Then laid they their hands on them, and they received the Holy Ghost.** [18]*And when Simon* **saw** *that through laying on of the apostles' hands the Holy Ghost was given, he offered them money* .... [20]*But Peter said unto him, your money perishes with thee, because you have thought that the gift of God may be purchased with money.* [21]*You have neither part nor lot in this* **matter (lit.; word):** *for your heart is not right in the sight of God.*

The record above states that one of the reasons Simon wanted to buy the ability to lay hands on people that they may receive the Holy Spirit was because he also heard "word." The Holy Spirit was specific here to use the word "logo" (word, exposed thought, expressed thought) and not "glossa" (tongues). This is found in Peter's correction to Simon. Peter stated that Simon had no "part nor lot in this **matter (Greek: logos, word)"** What "word?"

Simon could not have a part in imparting the **"word (lit., logos) of knowledge,"** or "the **word (lit., logos) of wisdom,"** or of **speaking** in tongues, or no part in imparting the manifestation of **prophesy,** or imparting the words of magnifying God, etc. Simon's heart was "not right in the sight of God" even though Simon claimed to have "believed" the gospel. Simon, the sorcerer, apparently believed; yet he was disqualified because of his attempt to merchandise the Holy Spirit through his bitterness and because his heart was not "immediate," "straight," or "well placed" with the Lord. We need the Holy Spirit as a confirming witness that Jesus indeed owns us. This occurs after our initial belief in Jesus.

Words are indeed heard as a confirmation that a Believer has the Spirit of Christ. Peter himself also declared that receiving the Spirit is witnessed by **sound** and **sight.** When the one hundred and twenty were filled with the Spirit, Peter declared that the experience could both be "seen" and "heard."[240] I believe what the observers in the book of Acts also saw relative to "sight," after seeing "tongues like fire" may be the sight of emotions displayed by the recipients of the Spirit of God.

When Jesus was filled after His baptism, John, the Baptist **"saw"** the Spirit descending **"in bodily shape like a dove."** [241] John saw a physical (bodily) form descend upon Jesus. Thus, experiencing the filling of the Holy Spirit may also be manifested by sight ("cloven tongues of fire"), and/or sound ("mighty rushing wind").

The point of saying all the above in this section is to demonstrate that we all need to be filled with the Holy Spirit. Why? According to the Scriptures, His indwelling in us is also needed to make us belong to Christ. Being filled with the Holy Spirit with evidence showing the filling is the **guarantee** that we belong to Jesus Christ.

*2 Corinthians 1:22: Who hath also **sealed** us, and given the **earnest (lit., pledge, guarantee, deposit)** of the Spirit **in** our hearts*

*2 Corinthians 5:5: Now he that hath wrought us for the selfsame thing is God, who also hath given unto us the **earnest of the Spirit**.*

Ephesians 1:13-14: [13]*In ... whom also after that you believed, you were **sealed with that Holy Spirit of promise,** [14]Which is the **earnest (lit., pledge, guarantee, deposit)** ... until the **redemption** of the **purchased possession,** unto the praise of his glory.*

*Romans 8:23: And not only they, but ourselves also, which have the **firstfruit of the Spirit,** even we ourselves groan within ourselves, waiting for the adoption, to wit, **the redemption of our body.***

The Spirit of Christ **in us** is the "pledge" that His "purchased possession" will be raised from the dead when Jesus comes. The infilling of the Holy Spirit moves us from the **"common salvation"**[242] (faith in Jesus) into the **"great salvation"**[243] (filled with Holy Spirit in demonstration and power) with the view of the **"eternal salvation"**[244] (eternal redemption).

This "eternal salvation" includes "the redemption of our body." When we have the Spirit of Christ, we are guaranteed to indeed belong to Christ. We who are Jesus' "purchased possession" through His blood are guaranteed of our inheritance by His Spirit in us "into the praise of His glory."

Thus, "in Christ all will be made alive. But each in his own turn: Christ, the firstfruit; then, when he comes, **those who belong to him.**"[245] In other words, we are secure in Him when we have been sealed in Him through the baptism of the Spirit of God. In fact, as many as have been baptized into Christ, have put on Christ. Because we put on Christ after baptism, we become Christ's. We also become heirs as the "seed" of Abraham, through Jesus Christ.

They That Are Christ Are Abraham's Seed

Galatians 3:26-29: [26]*For **you are all 'sons' of God by faith in Christ Jesus.** [27]For as many of you as have been **baptized into Christ have put on Christ.** [28]There is neither Jew nor Greek, there* is neither bond nor free, there is neither male nor female: for you are all one in Christ Jesus. ²⁹*And if you be Christ's, then are you Abraham's seed,* and heirs according to *the promise.*

1Corinthians 12:13: For by one Spirit are we all baptized into one body, whether [we be] Jews or Gentiles, whether [we be] bond or free; and have been all made to drink into one Spirit.

Abraham's seed also belongs to Christ. Faith in Christ makes us "sons of God."²⁴⁶ That is, those who are Abraham's seed through faith in Christ and through baptism of the Spirit into one body will partake of the resurrections because Abraham's seed (all of God's sons) "belongs to Christ." We become Abraham's seed by faith and being "baptized into Christ...."²⁴⁷

These are those who are made righteous through faith in Christ as Abraham was made righteous through faith in the Lord.²⁴⁸ These are those who belong to Christ by receiving "the promise of the Spirit through faith." These are those who will **inherit rulership of the world** through Jesus Christ as promised to Abraham and his seed.

Romans 4:13: For the promise, that he should be the heir of the world, was not to Abraham, or to his seed, through the law, but through the righteousness of faith.

Galatians 3:14: That the blessing of Abraham might come on the Gentiles through Jesus Christ; that we might receive the promise of the Spirit through faith.

Thus, the promise of becoming rulers of the world by **"inheritance"** is realized in the resurrection of the dead of Abraham's seed.²⁴⁹ Again for clarity, Abraham's seed consists of Jesus Christ and they that are baptized into Christ through the Holy Spirit by the hearing of faith. The Bible calls us "all the seed."²⁵⁰ Saying it another way, we who believe in Jesus

Christ receive "the promise of the Spirit" "by [the] faith of Jesus Christ."[251] Remember, it is the Spirit's baptism that makes us belong to Christ by faith.[252]

*Hebrews 10:38a: Now the **just (or righteous)** shall live **by faith (lit., by his faith).***

*Habakkuk 2:4a: ... but the **just (or righteous)** shall live by **his** faith.*

It is by His (Jesus') faith we become righteous. It is by His faith we become Abraham's seed. "The life which I now live in the flesh I live **by the faith of the Son of God,** who loved me, and gave himself for me."[253] Thus, we who are heirs of the world because we are Abraham's seed will rule with Christ (the Seed) in the first resurrection.

Resurrection is linked to perfected (matured) faith which Abraham also demonstrated. We should move from **"beginning"** faith or "common faith" to the place where we "live by the faith of the Son of God" — the **"finishing" faith.**[254] We move "from faith to faith."[255]

Part of the finishing faith is "... **the faith** of the **operation (energy)** of God, who hath **raised** [Jesus] from the dead."[256] It is the "perfected faith" that is developed by doing the "works" that God requires of us, as Abraham worked.[257] Abraham did indeed receive righteousness without works, the righteousness by faith. This is the faith that the Bible calls the "beginning faith" or the "common faith."[258] However, faithful Abraham also took his faith to maturity, the faith that is **perfected by works.** "Was not Abraham our father **justified by works**, when he had offered Isaac his son upon the altar? See you how faith wrought with his works, and **by works was faith made perfect?**"[259]

Romans 1:16-17: *[16]For I am not ashamed of the gospel of Christ.... For therein is the righteousness of God revealed **from faith to faith**: as it is written, the just shall live by faith.*

*Hebrews 12:2: Looking unto Jesus the **author (or beginning leader)** and **finisher (completer)** of our faith....*

Abraham's faith eventually reached the faith of raising the dead.[260] First we know that he "heard" God, because "faith comes by hearing." Second, we also know that he did the work that God asked him to do.[261] A person doing what God requires brings that person to perfected faith. Abraham was asked to offer up his only son.

Abraham went "from" the "faith;" from believing God for righteousness "to" the "faith" of believing God for the resurrection of the dead. He drew nearer to the perfect one (God) by obedience; and thus, his faith was perfected. Abraham became convinced of God's resurrection power. This faith to believe that God could raise the dead was also demonstrated by Abraham's work of offering up his only son Isaac, as God has commanded.

The Scriptures in the book of Hebrews, Chapter 11:17-19 said that Abraham believed that God would have raised Isaac (the promised seed) from the dead, if Isaac was indeed offered up on the altar. This kind of faith is what the Bible calls the "God kind of faith." The energy of God's faith that raised Jesus from the dead will also raise those who belong to Christ, because they are also Abraham's seed through faith.

The seed's "perfected faith" is the faith that believes there will be resurrection of the dead and resurrection of eternal judgment. As we go on to the Perfect One, we will be perfected (resurrected) by the faith of the son of God in us, "the faith of the energy of God" that raises the dead. Christ's seed through the Holy Spirit will rule the world as promised.[262] The faith of Jesus will "complete **our** faith" in Him by using the energy of His faith. This is the faith of God that will raise we who are Abraham's seed from the dead. We will reign with Christ through the power of the Holy Spirit.

The Resurrection of Eternal Judgment

John 5:28-29: [28]*Marvel not at this: for the hour is coming, in the which **all** that are **in the graves** shall hear his voice,* [29]*And shall come forth; they that have done good, unto the **resurrection of life;** and they that have done evil, unto the **resurrection of damnation** (**Greek, crisis**).*

*John 5:29, NAU: And will come forth; those who did the good deeds to a **resurrection of life**, those who committed the evil deeds to a **resurrection of judgment**.*

*John 5:29, YLT: And they shall come forth; those who did the good things to a **rising again of life**, and those who practiced the evil things to a **rising again of judgment**.*

*Hebrews 6:1-2: Therefore, leaving the principles of the doctrine of Christ, let us go on unto perfection; not laying again the foundation ... **of resurrection of the dead, and of eternal judgment**.*

There is a resurrection of the dead. There is also the resurrection of eternal judgment. The Greek for Hebrews 6:2 above reads as such: "...and of resurrection **both** of the dead and of eternal judgment." So, there is a resurrection **"both"**[263] of the (righteous) dead <u>and</u> a resurrection of eternal judgment.

This resurrection of eternal judgment is what our Lord declared to be the resurrection where **"all** that are in the graves shall hear His voice and shall come forth." Prior to this resurrection only a selected group (the saints) was raised. In this resurrection "all" the rest will be raised.

The resurrection of eternal judgment will be a "resurrection of **crisis"** for some who have **"practiced habitually"** evil. Yet the resurrection of eternal judgment will also be a resurrection of

life for others who have missed the first resurrection and yet have **"done good."** We know that Jesus' statement in John 5:28-29 is not necessarily referring to the first resurrection because Jesus indicated that **"all"**[264] in the grave would hear His voice and come forth. However, in the first resurrection, only **"part"**[265] of the dead will be raised.

The Resurrection of the Dead

The **"resurrection of the dead,"** as declared in Hebrews 6:2 includes those of **"the resurrection of the just."**[266] It will also include the **"better resurrection"** defined in Hebrews 11:35. This **"resurrection of the dead"** consists of the **courses in the first resurrection** (those the firstfruit Christ (the two witnesses), those "in Christ" who will be resurrected in Jesus' coming, the sitting judges, the beheaded souls and the ones who overcome the three beasts).

Following the "better resurrection," in "turn," there will be the resurrection of eternal judgment. The eternal judgment is the judgment when "all" the rest of the dead who were not a part of the first resurrection stand up before the Great White Throne.

Matthew 22:31-33: [31]*But as touching* **the resurrection of the dead,** *have you not read that which was spoken unto you by God, saying,* [32] *I am the God of Abraham, and the God of Isaac, and the God of Jacob?* **God is not the God of the dead, but of the living.** [33] *And when the multitude heard this,* **they were astonished at his doctrine.**

1 Corinthians 15:42-44: [42]*So also is* **the resurrection of the dead.** *It is sown in corruption; it is raised in incorruption:* [43]*It is sown in dishonor; it is raised in glory: it is sown in weakness; it is raised in power:* [44]*It is sown a natural body; it is raised a spiritual body. There is a natural body, and there is a spiritual body.*

"The resurrection of the dead" as scripturally defined above, is part of the first resurrection; because per Paul's discourse, **"the resurrection of the dead"** will be raised "in incorruption," "in glory," "in power," a "spiritual body," "life-producing," and "immortal." Jesus includes Abraham, Isaac, and Jacob among "the resurrection of the dead" in His discourse.

Thus, they are part of the first resurrection, regardless of which course of the first resurrection they were raised. Why? The God of Jesus is their God; He is a God of the living,[267] and they have the "good seed."[268] And, "God gives…to each **seed** its own body."[269] That is, the "seed" determines the body God gives to each person. We/they who believe in Jesus are of the good seed—Jesus Christ.

Resurrection of Eternal Judgment

The fourth resurrection mentioned by Paul in 1 Corinthians 15:23-24 is the resurrection of "conclusion."[270] This resurrection of "the end (finish)" is also called the **"resurrection…of eternal judgment,"** which is the resurrection from the graves, the sea, Death, and Hades of "all" the remaining dead. After the graves, the sea, Death, and Hades deliver up the dead who is in them, Death and Hell will also be punished with the eternal judgment. This will fulfill Paul's declaration that the last enemy to be destroyed is Death, which occurs after the resurrection of the "end."[271]

Some of the people who are raised from the dead in this resurrection will also be punished eternally **"if"** they are not found written in the Book of Life, if they have blasphemed the Holy Spirit, and if they have "practiced and personified the foul."[272] Again, this is what Jesus calls the "resurrection of damnation," which literally means "the resurrection of **crisis.**"

The **"crisis"** may include the possibility of not being found written in the Book of Life.

Revelation 20:5a: But the **rest of the dead** *lived not again until the thousand years were finished ....*

Revelation 20:11-15: ¹¹And I saw a great white throne, and him that sat on it, from whose face the earth and the heaven fled away; and there was found no place for them. ¹²And I saw **the dead,** *small and great,* **stand** *before God (lit., throne); and the books were opened: and another book was opened, which is the book of life: and the dead were judged out of those things which were written in the books, according to their works. ¹³And the* **sea gave up the dead** *which were in it; and* **death and hell delivered up the dead which were in them:** *and they were judged every man according to their works. ¹⁴And death and hell were cast into the lake of fire. This is the second death. ¹⁵***And whosoever was not found written in the book of life was cast into the lake of fire.***

Matthew 25:41: Then shall he say also unto them on the left hand, depart from me, you cursed, **into everlasting fire,** *prepared for the devil and his angels:*

Matthew 25:41 above describes what I believe to be <u>also</u> linked to the resurrection of eternal judgment because it is associated with "everlasting fire" ("the lake of fire"). If you have part in the first resurrection (including the resurrection at the coming of the Lord), the Scripture assures us that the second death, the lake of fire, has **"no 'authority'"** over us.

However, if one is not separated from the dead in the first resurrection, and/or in Jesus' physical coming, then deliverance from the lake of fire becomes acutely **conditional.** Thus, the resurrection of eternal judgment is "the resurrection of 'crisis'"²⁷³ for those not found written in the Book of Life. The Scripture states, "And **whosoever** was not found written in the book of life was cast into the lake of fire." This statement is conditional. The Greek reads, **"'if any'** was not found written in the Book of Life."

Thus, <u>an implicit</u> understanding is that some must have been found written in the Book of Life, even though they did not partake in the resurrection of the Just. These are the ones that have **"done good"** who still qualify for eternal life through the mercies of God. Please note that according to Strong's Concordance, the word "good" used in John 5:29 carries the idea of **a single act.** Thus, this shows the everlasting mercy of God that extends even to the resurrection of eternal judgment. He finds every way to save and to give life.

Those who have done good may also be some who call upon the name of Jesus to be saved. However, they did not make Jesus Lord or King of their lives. Saying it another way, these are they that believe that Jesus did indeed die for them but did not show their faith by making Jesus "Controller" of their lives.

Now notice, Revelation 20:15 did not say that **"all"** who stand in this judgment were not found written in the Book of Life. On the contrary, He said **"if any"** was not found written. Oh! The mercy of God! Remember, **If any** man's work shall be burned, he shall suffer loss: **but he himself shall be saved; yet so as by fire.**[274] They believed in Jesus and possessed the "common salvation" — their "work shall be burned" up by the fire; yet they "shall be saved."

They may not have partaken of the "great salvation" because of not being filled with the Holy Spirit. Some may not have **"obeyed"** God, thus their **"cause"** for being in the better resurrection of the **"eternal salvation"** was not **"asked for"** by Jesus.[275] **"If any"** was found written in the Book of Life at this resurrection, it is because Jesus must have also confessed their names from the Book of Life.[276]

During the resurrection of the eternal judgment, they will <u>also</u> be judged **"according to their works."** These works may be the **"good doings"** that Jesus referenced in John 5:29. And as indicated earlier, **If any** man's work shall be burned, he shall suffer loss: **but he himself shall be saved; yet so as by fire.**[277] In the eternal resurrection some will be judged according to their works out of the things written in the **"books."**

There is the book of wars[278] of the Lord (are you in the war?[279]). There is the book of the just or righteous (have you done any works of righteousness like Abraham[280]). There is the book of remembrance[281] (for those who fear him and think upon His name). There is the book of the Lord[282] (record of God's prophetic words that does not fail), and there are the books of the apostles, the prophets, and so on.

There is the Book of Life which is also **personified** in Jesus. He came "in the volume of the book."[283] Jesus is the personification of **God's Word "made flesh."**[284] Jesus is also the Life. Are you written in Him upon the table of His heart as exemplified in the breastplate of the high priest in the Old Testament? The priest had the names of the twelve tribes written on stones and carried on his chest. Thus, we are written in Jesus' heart, he is being the Book of Life, personified.

It follows that **the books** can also be personified as a people. The Church is "the epistle of Christ."[285] Paul stated that the saints are the **"criterion"** for judging the world and angels.[286] Paul declared that "You [the Saints] show that you are a letter from Christ."[287] Every time a person meets us, we are epistles "known and read by everybody."[288] The same will be true in the resurrection of eternal judgment. Those who belong to Christ will be as open books.

With that said, I would now like to turn my attention to another important question. When does eternal judgment really begin? According to the apostle Peter, judgment begins from the house of God, those who suffer as Christians. Our Lord Jesus, who is blessed for evermore, also demonstrated that some can be affected with eternal judgment in this life.

When Does Eternal Judgment Begin?

*Mark 3:29: But he who **blasphemes** against the Holy Spirit never has forgiveness but is subject to **eternal condemnation**.*

*Revelation 13:1: And I stood upon the sand of the sea and saw a beast 'up-step' out-of the sea ... and upon his heads **the name of blasphemy**.*

Jesus gives evidence that the eternal judgment appears to have **present** implications. Jesus implied this when He told the blasphemers of the Holy Spirit that they will never be forgiven for their blasphemy against the Holy Spirit; but one who does blaspheme against the Holy Spirit **"is" (present tense)** subject to eternal judgment. The Bible also gives other evidence that eternal judgment is executed before the last resurrection.

This is demonstrated in the beast and the false prophet. They were arrested in the book of Revelation and judged for their "sin onto death" — blasphemy. This will be a result of the "King of kings and the Lord of lords" making known the "only dynasty" — Jesus.'

The beast and the false prophet appear to be the first to go to the lake of eternal fire prepared for the devil and his angels. (All those who are considered as "goats" will also experience this eternal fire.[289]) The Scriptures through Paul also imply that the eternal **"judgment (Greek: krimatos)"** has already begun.

Thus, if this eternal judgment has begun from the days of Jesus, then it should not be strange that at the beginning of the millennium, during the millennium, and at the end there will be eternal judgment executed. The saints shall judge the world and angels.[290] This eternal judgment executed by the saints is based upon them being "seated"[291] to judge eternally. The angels that follow the devil are among those angels that will experience this eternal judgment.[292]

*Hebrews 6:1-2: Therefore, leaving the principles of the doctrine of Christ, let us go on unto perfection; not laying again the foundation ...of **resurrection**... **of eternal judgment.***

Judgment is translated from the Greek word "krimatos." **"Krimatos"** is only used one more place in the Bible. (Now bear with me, I will walk you through a little transliterated Greek to bring some clarity to this resurrection of eternal judgment.) I will cite a statement made by Luke concerning the Apostle Paul's witness to Felix.

*Acts 24:25: And as he (Paul) reasoned of righteousness, temperance, and **judgment (krimatos)** to come Felix trembled, and answered, go thy way for this time; when I have a convenient season, I will call for thee.*

Paul talked about this **"judgment (krimatos)** to come." Whatever he said it caused Felix to "tremble." Again, this word "krimatos" is an inflection of the Greek word "krima." We get our English word "crime" from "krima." The book of Hebrews calls this "krimatos" the "eternal krimatos." Again, Paul was the only other person to use this inflection (krimatos). The words **"to come"** are also of import.

The words "to come" in Acts 24:25 cited earlier is the Greek word **"méllo"** and it is "present tense" in Acts 24:25. The Jamieson, Fausset, and Brown Commentary indicate that the present tense of "mello," "as distinguished from the simple future, **denotes an action already begun,** or at least in preparation, **rather than wholly future."** It is an "impending" action. The phrase in Acts 24:25 can read **"judgment is impending (presently).**

Thus, eternal judgment appears to be at a point of execution presently. **That is, there may be some in this life that are making decisions that may have eternal implications.** Felix must have realized this, and thus trembled as Paul declared righteousness, self-control, and **judgment.** Maybe Felix for a moment realized that he was participating in actions that have negative eternal implications.

The Pharisees had also committed a sin that had eternal implications. This is the sin that the Bible calls a "sin unto death"[293] (the second death). The Pharisees had blasphemed the Holy Spirit. They thought that they could get away with that belief. Jesus shocked them! He held them to an eternal judgment. They would not be forgiven for blasphemy of the Holy Spirit. Thus, eternal judgment was declared upon them by Jesus.

Blasphemy Causes an Eternal Verdict

Mark 3:29-30, N: [29]*But he who* **blasphemes against the Holy Spirit never has forgiveness,** *but is subject to* **eternal condemnation** [30]*because they said, "He has an unclean spirit."*

Anyone who calls the Holy Spirit an unclean spirit commits a sin against the Holy Spirit that **"will never be forgiven."** Blasphemy against the Spirit is a sin that **cannot be prayed for;**[294] it is "a sin unto death" that puts into effect an eternal verdict (the second death) in this life. The Greek texts above read that **"he who blasphemes against the Holy Spirit is 'not holding forgiveness,' but is 'holding-in' eternal 'judgment;'** because they said, He has an unclean spirit."

The Pharisees who called the Holy Spirit an unclean spirit will not be forgiven into the age. Matthew was a little more assertive. He writes that blasphemy against the Holy Spirit "shall not be forgiven him, neither in this world,[295] and neither in the world to come." From the time that Jesus spoke those words to the Pharisees until the resurrection of the eternal judgment, they were already judged eternally.

"The age" that Jesus referred to is "the age to come" — the millennium rule of the **"seated"** saints **with** Christ. In "the age," the King of kings and the Lord of lords' dynasty will "appear upon" all. At that time, all who have committed the sin unto death will not be a part of the first resurrection. And for those who follow the three beasts by blaspheming the Spirit of God, they will be judged in righteousness in the King of kings and Lord of lords' appearing.

The Beast's Sin unto the Second Death

*Revelation 13:1, 5, 6: And I stood upon the sand of the sea and saw a beast 'up-step' out-of the sea...and upon his heads **the name of blasphemy.** ⁵And there was given unto him a mouth speaking great things and blasphemies...⁶And he opened his mouth in **blasphemy against God,** to **blaspheme his name,** and **his tabernacle,** and **them that dwell in heaven.***

The beast is a blasphemer. He blasphemes God, and we know that God is Spirit.[296] Thus, the beast is saying that the work of the Lamb and the saints are being done through an unclean spirit. Or, he is calling God, unclean. This "blasphemy" is what Jesus says results in eternal judgment.

This blasphemy of the Spirit of God is dangerous and has other stems. For example, men have even gone as far as to call speaking in tongues (a manifestation of the Holy Spirit) a characteristic of demons. They have indeed blasphemed the Holy Spirit.

"The Spirit is truth"[297] is "the Holy Spirit," because He is literally "the 'Clean' Spirit." The Holy Spirit is God. Thus, if one blasphemes and calls the Holy Spirit, unclean, that person must have "the spirit of error (lit., wandering)." The spirit of error is the spirit of the false prophet. Thus, the Pharisees and Sadducees[298] of today who reject the infilling of the Holy Spirit are of the spirit of the false prophet.

The false prophet, the spirit of error, is very present in this generation. It blasphemes and opposes all that is called God (i.e., true miracles, true healings, speaking in tongues, "apostles of Christ," prophets, and the like) or all that is worshiped as the true and living God. Thus, the King of kings does not hesitate to judge the dragon, false prophet, and the beast in His appearing.

It was the false prophet and the beast that were among the first to go the lake of fire. Why? They committed the sin unto the second death (the eternal judgment). One of the reasons for them being eternally judged is the beast blasphemed God and the beast's very name (nature) is blasphemy. Also, the false prophet was the entity that deceived people to take on the name of the beast, which is blasphemy.

Revelation 13:11-12; 17: [11]*And I beheld **another beast** coming up out of the earth; and he had two horns like a lamb, and he spoke, as a dragon.* [12]*And he exercises all the power of the first beast before him and causes the earth and them which dwell therein to worship the first beast...* [17]**And that no man might buy or sell,** *save he that had the mark, or the **name of the beast,** or the number of his name.*

The beast and the false prophet committed the unpardonable sin; they blasphemed God. **They also caused others to take on this name of blasphemy by** **economic pressure.** **"No man**

might buy or sell, save he that had the mark, or the name of the beast, or the number of his name."

The beast and the false prophet were eventually judged with the eternal fire—the eternal judgment—for their practices. This appears to be done either directly before the one thousand years rule or just into the start of the millennium rule of the resurrected saints with Christ.

*Revelation 19:20: And the beast was taken, and with him the false prophet that wrought miracles before him, with which he deceived them that had received the mark of the beast, and them that worshipped his image. **These both were cast alive into a lake of fire burning with brimstone.***

Eternal Verdicts

The "eternal judgment" consists of eternal "verdicts." There is the punishment of eternal decay. There is the verdict of eternal fire or eternal punishment, and so on. Eternal punishment is also associated with eternal fear.

*2 Thessalonians 1:7-10: [7]And to you who are troubled rest with us, when the Lord Jesus shall be revealed from heaven with his mighty angels, [8]In flaming fire **taking vengeance on them that know not God, and** that **obey not the gospel** of our **Lord** Jesus Christ: [9]Who shall be punished with **everlasting destruction (or, eternal decay)** from the presence of the Lord, and from the glory of his power; [10]When he shall come to be glorified **in his saints,** and to be admired in all them that believe (because our testimony among you was believed) in that day.*

The Scriptures above provide another indication that eternal verdicts will also occur prior to the resurrection of eternal judgment. Christ will be **"uncovered"** to be glorified **"in"** His saints to administer "vengeance."

*Jude 1:14-15: And Enoch also, the seventh from Adam, prophesied of these, saying, Behold, the **Lord comes with (lit., in)** ten thousands of his **saints**, to execute judgment upon all....*

When Jesus comes **"in"**[299] His Saints, those **who do not know God,** and those who have **not obeyed the gospel** of our Lord Jesus Christ will be punished with **"eternal decay."** According to the book of First John, those who do not know God are those who do not do "His commandments (lit., directions)."

*1 John 2:3-4: ³And **hereby we do know that we know him** if we **keep his commandments.** ⁴He that saith, I know him, and keeps not his commandments, is a liar, and the truth is not in him.*

God's commands are for us to love God and love our brothers and sisters in Christ.[300] Saying it another way: according to John, those who **"love"** are those who actually know God.[301] Thus, there will be an eternal punishment for not loving God. Without love we are nothing.[302]

Obeying the gospel of Jesus Christ is also important. This basically means that the nations did not accept the "gospel of their salvation" offered through Jesus Christ; and they also did not accept the "Lordship" (control) of Jesus over their lives. They did not accept Jesus' justification by faith.[303] The result of not knowing God and not obeying the gospel of our Lord Jesus Christ is eternal decay. The fact that the decay is "eternal" puts this judgment in the class of eternal judgment. This is the decay that never ceases from decaying.

*Mark 9:43-44: ⁴³...It is better for thee to enter into life maimed, than having two hands to go into hell, into the fire that never shall be quenched: ⁴⁴Where their **worm dies not,** and the fire is not quenched.*

*Isaiah 66:24: And they shall go forth and look upon the **carcasses** of the men that have transgressed against me: for their **worm shall*** *not die, neither shall their fire be quenched; and they shall be an abhorring unto all flesh.*

The worms that eat flesh at death will never die on these decaying bodies. They will be in an eternal state of decaying, yet never dying, being eaten by **eternal worms ("worms that die not").** May as many people as possible get to know the God of Jesus and reverence Him! May all obey Him! **God is love and His delight is mankind!** His Word says that God does not take pleasure in the death of the wicked.[304]

It is God's "will to have all men to be saved and come unto the knowledge of the truth."[305] Thus, I hope all may come to obey the gospel of our Lord Jesus Christ! I hope all submit to His ruler-ship! I hope that no one sends ambassadors after Jesus saying, "they do not want Him to rule over them!" Thus, I hope many through God's mercy be delivered from "the fire that cannot be quenched" — the eternal fire.

Eternal Fire Was <u>Not</u> Intended for Mankind

The Scriptures also talk of eternal fire, which the Bible also calls eternal punishment. The eternal fire was originally prepared for the devil and his angels. **God did not have us in mind when He made this eternal fire.** Thus, mankind does not have to experience the eternal judgment, if they become His "sheep." When the Son of man sits on the throne of His glory, he shall separate the sheep from the goats.[306] The goats shall be punished in the same place the devils will be punished.

Matthew 25:41, 46: [41]*Then shall he say also unto them on the left hand, depart from me, you cursed, into **everlasting fire,** prepared for the devil and his angels...*[46]*And these shall go away into **everlasting punishment:** but the righteous into life eternal.*

The eternal fire was <u>not</u> intended for mankind. It was for the devil and his angels.[307] It was after the fall of man that mankind became subjected to this eternal punishment. Apparently, these "goats" who led themselves to the lake of fire must have acted like the devil and are thus **punished** with devils.

This word **"punishment"** is used one other place in the Scriptures. It is used of the punishment of fear.[308] Thus, there will be eternal fear with the eternal fire. As indicated earlier, this is for those who were not "sheep."

Matthew 25:32-46: *32And before him [the King] shall be gathered **all nations:** and he shall separate them one from another, as a shepherd divides his **sheep** from the **goats:** 33And he shall set **the sheep on his right hand,** but the **goats on the left** ...41Then shall he say also unto **them on the left** hand, depart from me, you cursed, into **everlasting fire,** prepared for the devil and his angels...46And these shall go away into **everlasting punishment:** but the righteous into life eternal.*

Let the Church of Jesus <u>remain</u> as Jesus' sheep. Let the nations <u>become</u> the sheep of Jesus. Let the nations visit the prisoners; let the nations feed the hungry; let the nations heal and visit the sick; let the nations take in the strangers; let the nations give water to the thirsty; and let the nations clothe the naked.

These lists of people (the sick, the hungry, the thirsty, and so on) are all brothers of Jesus. Jesus also stated that doing well to these "brothers" of His is like doing well to Jesus Himself. In Acts 9, The Lord made a similar statement to Paul when Paul was persecuting the Church before the Lord saved him.

Matthew 25:37-40: *37Then shall the righteous answer him, saying, Lord, **when** saw we thee hungry, and fed thee, or thirsty, and gave thee drink? 38When saw we thee a stranger, and took thee in, or naked, and clothed thee? 39Or **when** saw we **thee** sick, or in prison,* *and came unto thee?* *40And the King shall answer and say unto them, Verily I say unto you, inasmuch as you have done it unto **one of the least of these my brethren, you have done it unto me.***

Matthew 25:40 above gives the name of people whom the nations are to treat well. They are to do the good works to the King's **brethren.** The hungry, the stranger, the sick, the naked, the prisoners, etc. were all the King's brethren. Therefore, the way the nations treat the brothers of Jesus has eternal implications.

Remember, the poor man Lazarus with his sores and the rich man who refused to help him.[309] The rich man who refused to help Lazarus was sent to Hades in torment; while Lazarus was carried personally by an angel to Abraham's bosom and so lived in comfort.

Remember also that the resurrection of the just are for the "blessed"[310] that helped people who could not repay them. The "blessed" will be repaid in the resurrection of the just at the judgment seat of Christ. The "blessed" also has course in the first resurrection.

Six Paces to the Judgment Seat, the Great White Throne

*Revelation 20:11-12: 11And I saw **a great white throne**, and **him that sat on it**, from whose face the earth and the heaven fled away; and there was found no place for them. 12And I saw the dead, small and great, stand before God (lit., the throne); and the books were opened: and another book was opened, which is the book of life: and the dead were judged out of those things which were written in the books, according to their works.*

When are the great white throne judgments? Can the saints ascertain the times and seasons of Jesus' judgments? The saints must appear before **"the judgment seat of Christ,"**[311] which is prior to the resurrection of eternal judgment. In fact, the Greek tense in 2 Corinthians 5:10 where "the judgment seat of Christ" is used indicates that the saints appearing before the judgment seat of Christ is a past action with ongoing actions and results (aorist tense[312]). Yet Romans 14:10 makes the appearance before the judgment seat future. Therefore, appearing before the judgment seat is a present reality and it will occur **when the Lord comes** (I Corinthians 4:5).

"Judgment seat" is also translated as "a place to set the foot on" (a footstool) in Acts 7:5. This is significant as we will see in a moment relative to the footstool of the Great White Throne and the resurrections. The resurrection of eternal judgment took place at the "Great White Throne."

The "judgment seat of Christ" is also at this same Great White Throne as can be seen in Solomon's throne. Solomon also had a **"great ivory throne."** Ivory, as you know, is basically "white" or cream in color. Thus, Solomon's "great ivory throne," before it was overlaid with "pure gold" was a type of the Great White Throne, **ivory being whitish.**

2 Chronicles 9:17-19: [17]*Moreover the king made a **great throne of ivory and** overlaid it with **pure gold.** [18]And there were **six steps to the throne,** with **a footstool** of gold, which were fastened to the throne, and stays on each side of the sitting place, and two lions standing by the stays:* [19]*And twelve lions stood there on the one side and on the other upon the six steps. There was not the like made in any **kingdom.***

As seen above, "ivory" is mentioned in the throne of Solomon. Thus, underneath the "pure gold" is **"white" ivory;** and as indicated, Solomon's throne typifies the Great White Throne where our Lord Jesus Christ and those who overcome to sit with Him in His throne.[313] issues judgments,

The **"gold"** that overlaid Solomon's great ivory [white] throne is a symbol of **"glory"** as defined in the New Testament.[314] This is also significant relative to Matthew 25:31 "when the Son of man shall come in His glory…then shall He sit upon the **throne of His glory."**

Solomon's great ivory throne was also **the throne of Solomon's glory** because it was overlaid with **"pure gold" (pure glory).** When Jesus ("the King") mentioned the **throne of His glory,** He also declared that the "sheep" from the nations would inherit the **"kingdom"** prepared for them from the foundation of the world.

With that said, in the writer's description of Solomon's throne, the writer was careful to mention that Solomon's throne was unique in any **"kingdom."** Thus, he placed Solomon's throne as a **"kingdom"** of God principle.

In Solomon's throne there was also a footstool of gold for his throne. The Hebrew word (כבש (KBSh)) translated as "footstool" is also translated as "lamb" in Leviticus 9:3 and Ezekiel 46:13.

Leviticus 9:3: And unto the children of Israel you shall speak, saying, take you a kid of the goats for a sin offering; and a calf and a **lamb (כבש (KBSh)),** *both of the first year, without blemish, for a burnt offering.*

Ezekiel 46:13: You shall daily prepare a burnt offering unto the LORD of **lamb (כבש (KBSh))** *of the first year without blemish: you shall prepare it every morning.*

Therefore, the verse in 2 Chronicles 9:18 could read:

"And there were **six steps to the throne,** *with a 'lamb' (כבש (KBSh)) of gold [glory]."*

Thus, at the Footstool (Bema) of Christ, there is the Lamb in glory that was slain for us, as pictured in Revelation 5:6. "And I beheld, and, lo, **in the midst of the throne** ... **stood a Lamb as it had been slain**, having seven horns and seven eyes," which are, "the Seven Spirits of God sent forth into all the earth."

Solomon's great ivory throne with its footstool is a type of the Great White Throne with its judgment (bema) seat of Christ where we must all appear before the **glorified Lamb** who takes away our sin. When Jesus appears "out of the second" for us, he will appear apart from sin.[315]

With that understood, "Judgment seat (Greek, bema)," straight from the Greek means a "step," "foot-breath;" the root is defined as "a foot." Judgment seat is translated in Acts 7:5 as "to set (foot) on." Thus, the judgment seat of Christ is the place where Christ set His foot on. Heaven is indeed His Throne. Yet remember that "the earth...is His footstool,[316] thus all the judgments in all the resurrections take place on the "earth" at His footstool.

Relative to the potential time(s) that the resurrected saints will appear before the judgment seat of Christ, Solomon's great ivory (white) throne also provided a glimpse into times and seasons, no exact date to mankind, just approximations. The approximate times to the footstool of Christ are **"six steps** to the throne" — "And there were **six steps to the throne, with a footstool** (Lamb) of gold (glory)."[317] Thus, Revelation 5:6 with the "throne" and the Lamb in the midst of the throne can be referenced in time to be approximately six thousand years from Adam.

The times to the judgment seat of Christ, which is part of the Great White Throne, are approximately **six "journeys to a higher place."** That is, it may take approximately six thousand years of journey from the fall of Adam to reach the "elevation" of the Throne of Jesus' glory, the Great White Throne. He who sits on the Great White Throne <u>may</u> manifest His judgments at the end of six millenniums as the "sons of the resurrection" are also seated <u>with</u> Christ. Now note: If one were to climb the steps of Solomon's throne, that person would get to the footstool (the Lamb) first, **"six steps to the throne, with a footstool (Lamb)."**

Thus, it is possible that approximately six thousand years from the first Adam, we all must appear before the judgment seat (footstool) of Christ, the Lamb. We will appear before the judgment seat of Christ to give an account to God concerning the practices done in the body, whether they were good or bad. Again, according to 1 Corinthians 4:5, this will occur when the Lord comes.

However, **at His judgment seat there will also be grace for Jesus' followers.** Remember the **glorified Lamb** is there **"in the middle of the throne,"** and the Lamb is the footstool there for our propitiation. "The Lamb of God takes away sin ...."[318] God in His mercy shall seek to praise those who accepted Jesus Christ, the Lamb of God. Jesus, the Lamb of God "He Himself is the propitiation (lit., Mercy Seat) for our sins, and not for ours only but also for the whole world;" and Jesus was raised by the glory of the Father for our justification.

Mercy and Praise at the Judgment Seat of Christ

---

1 Corinthians 4:5: Therefore, judge nothing before the time, **until the Lord come,** *who both will bring to light the hidden things of darkness and will make manifest the counsels of the hearts: and* **then shall every man have praise of God.**

When the Lord comes to judge and make manifest the counsels of the hearts **"every man shall have praise of**

God."[319] This "praise of God" may sound strange to some. However, for those whom God has granted repentance; and since He has forgiven our sins and iniquities unconditionally, there is good expectation. Unto those who look for His Jesus, our High Priest "shall appear 'out of' the second apart from sin 'into' salvation."[320]

God does not remember our sins.[321] All believers who are made **peacemakers through the Lord, who are made holy by the name of Jesus and the Holy Spirit, and those who fear the Lord**[322] will receive praise according to what was practiced in the body. Everyone who is circumcised in spirit by the Lord shall receive **"praise...of God."**[323] Listen to Zephaniah, "The Lord thy God in the midst of thee [is] mighty; he will save, **he will rejoice over thee with joy;** he will rest in his love, **he will joy over thee** with singing."[324]

However, for those who draw back from God, and hide their secret works of lawlessness from God, I am not sure of the outcome. What I am sure about is that any sin that is confessed and asked to be forgiven, God forgives them, except for one sin as we learned earlier.

Thus, never hide from God or attempt to hide any sin from the Father. The Scripture says He is faithful and just to forgive you of any sin that you confess to Him.[325] He does not remember your sins once you are forgiven; and in that day when He comes, you will have praise of God. Now that's good news!

After the saints are manifested at His judgment seat, His rule from His throne, which began when He ascended to the right hand of God after His resurrection,[326] continues into the day that has no end. His rule and judgments will continue to manifest even unto the "resurrection ... of the eternal judgment."

Jesus will put down the last ruling enemies—Death and Hades—after the resurrection of eternal judgment. "Then cometh the end, when he shall have delivered up the kingdom to God, even the Father; when he shall have put down all rule and all authority and power....And when all things shall be subdued unto him, then shall the Son also himself be subject unto him that put all things under him **that God may be all in all**"[327]

Prayer opportunity:

If you are not sure if you will partake of any of the resurrections prior to the resurrection of eternal judgment, here is a prayer you can pray. "I confess with my mouth that the Lord Jesus is the Christ; and I believe in my heart that Jesus died for my sins and that God has raised Jesus from the dead for my justification. Because, in my heart I believe that Jesus is the Christ unto righteousness and with my mouth, confession is made unto salvation." Amen! *(See 1 John 5:1 w/Rom 10:9-10)*

Name of the person praying: _____

Date and Time of Prayer: _____

End Notes

[1] John 5:28-29

[2] A phrase used by the late Dr. Kelley Varner when teaching on the resurrection from the book of Ruth. (He was a mentor to me for ~15 years, who became like a father to me for ~4 years before his passing).

[3] 1 Corinthians 15:20-27.

[4] 1 Corinthians 15:20; Matthew 28:1-7

[5] 1 Corinthians 15:23b, Revelation 20:1-6

[6] 1 Corinthians 15:23c w/1 Thessalonians 4:13-16

[7] 1 Corinthians 15:24a ("end" is defined as "conclusion," "termination," etc.); Hebrews 6:2

[8] Hebrews 6:2

[9] Hebrews 6:1-2 w/John 5:29; Revelation 20:5 w/Revelation 20:12-13

[10] Matthew 27:52-53

[11] John 5:39-40

[12] Matthew 28:6

[13] Matthew 22:29

[14] Matthew 28:6

[15] Luke 20:36

[16] Luke 20:35

[17] John 11:24

[18] 2 Pet 3:8

[19] 2 Peter 3:8 indicates that one day with the Lord is as a thousand years and a thousand years is as one day. Jesus came four thousand years (or according to 2nd Peter, four days) after Adam was made in the earth. We are now two thousand years (or two days according to Peter) from when Jesus came. The seventh one thousand years from the first Adam is about to begin.

[20] 1 Corinthians 15:45

[21] "Part" in Revelation 20:6 is translated as "course" in 1 Corinthians 14:27

[22] 1 Corinthians 15:22-23

[23] 1 Corinthians 15:20

[24] Colossians 2:18

[25] Matthew 27:52

[26] Colossians 1:18

[27] James 1:18 declared that those who were "some" of the firstfruit existed in James' days.

[28] Hebrews 6:1-2

[29] John 5:29: Per Strong's Concordance "done" in the phrase "done good" carries the idea of a single act; however, this word "done" (poiesantes) is nominative and therefore "personified;" the Greek word for "done" (praxantes) in "done evil" is also nominative and personified.

[30] There are some who are "liable" to "eternal judgment" if they have committed blasphemy as defined by Jesus in Mark 3:28-29 w/Mark 3:22-27; see also Revelation 13.

[31] John 5:28-28

[32] Matthew 5:16, Titus 3:8, Titus 3:14, John 10:32, Acts 9:36, Eph 2:10, 1 Tim 5:10, 1 Tim 5:25, Titus 2:7, Hebrews 10:24, 1 Per 2:12, James 2:17-26

[33] Compare 2 Corinthians 12:1-3

[34] Job 26:14

[35] Job 26:7

[36] Job 26:7

[37] Job 26:8

[38] Job 26:11

[39] Job 26:12

[40] Job 26:13

[41] Job 26:14

[42] Matthew 24:36; Matthew 25:13

[43] In all the Greek text "firstfruit" is singular

[44] 1 Tim 1:1; 1 John 3:2-3; Ezekiel 37:11-14

[45] Romans 5:15; 18

[46] John 11:25-26

[47] John 11:25, New King James

[48] John 17:1-3

[49] 2 Pet 1:19

[50] Isaiah 26:19

[51] Job 14:13-15

[52] John 10:35

[53] Romans 4:25

[54] Dan 9:24

[55] Isa 53:11

[56] 2 Pet 1:19

[57] John 1:14; 1 John 4:2

[58] John 5:39

[59] Matthew 21:38

[60] Matthew 28:12-15

[61] Matthew 26:60-61 w/ Matthew 27:63-64

62 Hebrews 7:8

63 Luke 24:36-46

64 James 2:14-26

65 Philippians 3

66 Luke 24:39

67 Acts 7:58-60

68 Deuteronomy 17; Deut. 22, Acts 7:58-60

69 1 Peter 4:6; 1 Peter 3:19

70 Luke 20:37

71 Romans 10:17; Hebrews 11

72 Matthew 11:11

73 Scholars differ on the interpretation of the Scripture *"For wherever the carcass (Gk.: ptoma) is, there the eagles will be gathered together" (Matthew 24:28, NKJ)*. Some believes Jesus' allegory alluded to Revelation 19:17-20 concerning Jesus' coming and the birds of mid-heaven (eagles, hawks, vultures; and so on) feeding of the corpse of the slain; while some believe that Jesus' used the example to show how believers will gather to Him as eagles to a corpse when He returns. Can both principles apply?

74 John 10:41

75 The "power of Elijah" also has implications relating to the corporate Elijah Ministry to manifest in the earth.

76 According to Luke 1:17, the of Elijah in John, the Baptist life related to turning heart of the fathers to children

77 Matthew 27:52-53

78 According to Luke 1:17, the of Elijah in John, the Baptist life related to turning heart of the fathers to children

79 Matthew 11:13; Luke 16:16

80 Matthew 14:12-13

81 John 8:52

82 Luke 16:19-31; 1 Pet 3:18-20; 1 Pet 4:6

83 Isaiah 44:1-2, Gen 32:31-32 w/Deuteronomy 32:15; 33:5; 33:26

84 Ezekiel 32:17-32

85 1 Peter 3:19

86 Matthew 27:52-53

87 Colossians 1:18

88 Acts 2:24, NIV; Matthew 27:52

89 2 Corinthians 4:13-14

[90] "Christ the firstfruits," in this verse, literally reads "firstfruit Christ." "Firstfruit" is *singular* in the Greek texts and in all the places it is used in the King James Version.

[91] Bishop Joel Thomas of Canada gave me this definition few years ago.

[92] Acts 11:26

[93] Romans 16:15; James 1:18, Revelation 14

[94] Revelation 11:11

[95] Col 1:18

[96] 1 Corinthians 15:20; Leviticus 23:10 w/23:5-9

[97] Jesus' male bond-slaves **and** female bond-slaves (Acts 2:18)

[98] Jews and Gentiles in one body (Romans 11)

[99] Sons who supply the Spirit to the Church (Zechariah 3:1-4:14)

[100] Witness of the prophetic Churches

[101] Prophets in the Spirit of Jesus (Moses) & the Spirit of John (Elijah)

[102] Acts 17:11

[103] 1 Corinthians 15:20

[104] A mature man by Scriptural definition is a man of love. Saying, it another way if a person does not walk in love, that person is immature.

[105] Romans 8:2; Revelation 11:11

[106] 1 Corinthians 15:41-42

[107] Revelation 20:6

[108] John 7:30; Revelation 11:7

[109] Revelation 11:19 w/ Revelation 10:7

[110] Greek word "kairos," which means: opportune time, season, set time, set occasion

[111] 1 Peter 4:6

[112] Revelation 10:6-7

[113] Act 4:33 w/Revelation 11:15-**17**

[114] Luke 10:21

[115] 1 Corinthians 3:16

[116] Colossians 1:27

[117] Numbers 17:8, last part

[118] 1 Thessalonians 4:15-16

[119] Matthew 24:20-21 w/Revelation 11:7

[120] Hebrews 5:4

[121] Revelation 11:19 w/Hebrews 9:4

[122] Frank Seekin has published outstanding materials on *Hebrew Word Pictures*.

123 Note: the vowels are not used in these Hebrew "base" words for simplicity

124 Vowels not shown for simplicity; and vowels were not utilized in ancient Hebrew texts as they are used in modern Hebrew

125 Vowels not shown for simplicity; and vowels were not utilized in ancient Hebrew texts as they are used in modern Hebrew

126 Compare Ruth's (type of the Church) one night with Boaz (type of Jesus) that changed her into another person.

127 Hebrews 12:23, "firstborn" is plural in the Greek and also means "first to produce."

128 1 Corinthians 15:28

129 See Revelation 11

130 The "soul" is associated with worry concerning clothing, eating, drinking, desires of the flesh (see Matthew 6:25-34, Luke 12:19 w/Luke 12:15-32 where "life" is literally "soul")

131 Genesis 37:3-4 w/Luke 3:22

132 John 15:25

133 Genesis 37:20 w/Acts 2:27

134 Genesis 37:28

135 Philippians 2:7

136 Gen 39:10-20 w/Matt 26:60

137 Matthew 26:60-64

138 Psalms 105:19

139 James 3:14-15, 1 Corinthians 2:14; Jude 1:19

140 Luke 20:35 w/2 Thessalonians 1:4-5

141 1 Thessalonians 3:3

142 Acts 14:22

143 Daniel 7 w/Dan 2

144 Revelation 13, Revelation 17:10, etc.

145 Daniel 7:7 w/Dan 7:17; Revelation 17:3 w/Revelation 17:9-10

146 1 Peter 2:17

147 1 Peter 2:13

148 Revelation 13:4; 13:7; 17:14; 19:19

149 I make this statement not being antimilitary; I served7 ½ years in the USMC.

150 Revelation 13:11-17

151 Revelation 13:11-17

152 Blasphemy, the name of the beast, also means to hinder fame.

153 Matthew 24:36-37, 1 Peter 3:15-16 w/1 Peter 3:3-14

[154]The Lord does come as a thief only to those in darkness (1 Thessalonians 5:4 w/5:2); however, the sons of light are given to know the times (plural) and seasons (plural) (1 Thessalonians 5:1-4. With that said, it was not given to us to predict the exact day or hour of Jesus' coming (mark 13:32). **It is foolish to predict the exact date (year, month, and day) of Jesus' coming.**

[155] 2 Peter 3:8

[156] Ephesians 2:19-22

[157] 1 Samuel 17

[158] Goliath "span" may also prophetically show that his arrogancy affected the "span" of the heaven (1 Samuel 17:4 w/Isaiah 40:12)

[159] Matthew 24:36-37

[160] Matthew 24:36-37

[161] 1 Kings 6:37-38: Solomon started building the temple in the 4th year of his reign in the 2nd month (Ziff or Ziv); and he completed in the 11th year in eighth month (Bul); thus 11-4=7, plus six months after Ziff, which is Bul. Thus, it took 7 ½ years to build.

[162] Jesus also started building His Church (the Temple of God) the fourth (4th) millennium from Mr. and Mrs. Adam. Also, the Passover Lamb was selected on the 10th day of the month, and four days later it was offered up for the sins of the people; so, Jesus Christ waited four (4) days [four (4) thousand years] to manifest as the Lamb of God to be slain for our sins and raised for our justification.

[163] 2 Chronicles 5:13-14. Note: according to 2 Chronicles 5:3, this occurred "in the feast which was in the seventh month;" and the Feat of Tabernacle occurred towards the middle of the 7th month.

[164] Ephesians 2:21 clearly states that there will be "generations of **'the age'** of-the ages. "The age" is related to the Holy of Holies; and thus, related to the millennium rule of Christ, His resurrected saints with Him (Hebrews 6:19-20). Therefore, there will be a continuation of generations in "the age to come."

[165] 1 Kings 7:23-26 w/2 Chronicles 4:2-6, w/Revelation 15:2-4 shows that around the 1400s, God began to reestablish Jesus' righteousness by washing His royal priesthood in the molten sea from the doctrines of the beast system. This washing from the influence of the beast will continue "until" complete cleansing from man's system. John Wycliffe's (1328 to 1384) teaching was one of the first steps to begin washing the priesthood from false doctrines. John Wycliffe taught reliance on Christ's suffering; and that believers are only justified by Jesus' righteousness. (The priests on the sea of glass mingled with fire were victorious "out of" the beast's

influences because of the "manifestation of [Jesus'] righteousness.") John Wycliffe is also the first to translate the Bible into English. We are washed in the water of the Word!

166 Romans 3:21

167 Ecclesiastes 3:19

168 The beast and the false prophet are the only ones who will go to the lake of fire before the millennium starts and before the resurrection of eternal judgment (Revelation 19:20).

169 1 Corinthians 6:20; Matthew 27:6; Colossians 1:20

170 I recommend that the reader reads all the book of Galatians.

171 Romans 14:1-3

172 1 Tim 4:4-5

173 1 Timothy 3:8; Matthew 11:19

174 1 Corinthians 11:21-22

175 Micah 2:11; Romans 14 is excellent regarding this topic.

176 1 Corinthians 10:29-33 w/Romans 14:6; 14:21-22

177 1 Timothy 5:23; 1 Corinthians 11:21-22; Romans 14:14 w/14: 17 w/14:20-21; Ps 104:14-15

178 Matthew 12:1-8; Luke 14:3-6

179 Galatians 4:10-11

180 Galatians 5:4

181 Luke 20:46-47

182 Hebrews 10:1

183 1 John 4

184 1 Corinthians 12:12; 2 Corinthians 3:6

185 Romans 3:23-25

186 Ephesians 2:9

187 1 John 5:1; Matthew 16:16-18

188 Romans 3:25, "propitiation" means "propitiatory shelter" or "mercy seat."

189 The word "propitiation" in Romans 3:25 is also translated as mercy seat in Hebrews 9:5.

190 Matthew 13:44-46

191 1 John 5:7-8

192 Romans 6:6

193 Matthew 16:24

194 Galatians 5:19-21

195 Galatians 5:15

196 Galatians 5:16, Romans 8:6

197 2 Corinthians 10:2-6
198 Galatians l 5:1
199 Romans 8:13
200 Romans 8:13-14
201 James 1:15
202 1 John 2:1
203 1 John 1:8-9
204 1 Thessalonians 4:4
205 Romans 8:2; Revelation 11:11
206 1 John 2:20; 24-26
207 Lit.: "'if much' of the Spirit of God dwells in you...." Thus, all saints should be "filled" by His Spirit, as a requirement that accompany salvation.
208 Acts 2:36
209 Acts 10:45
210 1 Corinthians 1:12-13
211 1 Corinthians 4:6-7
212 1 John 5:6-7
213 Ephesians 1:13-14
214 Ephesians 1:13-14
215 Greek "te" means "both" and "also."
216 Acts 2:6, "language" is "dialect" in the Greek.
217 I Corinthians 12:10, Acts 2:6
218 1 Corinthians 12:10, Acts 19:6, Luke 1:67
219 Acts 10:46, 1 Corinthians 12:3
220 1 Corinthians 12:6, Acts 8:21, Luke 1:41-43
221 2 Corinthians 4:13; Romans 10:6
222 Galatians 5:22-23
223 1 Corinthians 13:1-2; 1 John 3:18
224 Romans 8:15
225 1 Corinthians 12:5 w/12:7-11
226 Galatians 5:22-23
227 Luke 1:15
228 1 John 5:6
229 Romans 8:16
230 Romans 11:33
231 Romans 11:33
232 1 Corinthians 13:1
233 1 Corinthians 14:5

[234] 1 Corinthians 12:30 in the NAU Bible also reads like the Greek texts: "…All do not speak in tongues do they…?

[235] Romans 8:15-16

[236] Mark 16:17

[237] Romans 8:15

[238] 1 Corinthians 12:3

[239] Luke 1:67

[240] Acts 2:33, Revelation 1:12

[241] John 1:32 w/Luke 3:22

[242] Jude 3

[243] Hebrews 2:3

[244] Hebrews 5:9

[245] I Corinthians 15:22-23, NIV

[246] Galatians 4:6-7; Romans 8:14-23

[247] Galatians 3:26-27 w/1 Corinthians 12:13

[248] Genesis 15:6

[249] Galatians 3:29 w/Romans 4:13, Revelation 11:15 w/Gen 14:19

[250] Romans 4:16

[251] Gal 3:22 w/Gal 3:14

[252] 1 Corinthians 12:13

[253] Galatians 2:20

[254] Hebrews 12:2

[255] Romans 1:17

[256] Colossians 2:12

[257] James 2:21-22

[258] Titus 1:4

[259] James 2:21-22, "perfect" is literally translated as "mature." Thus, our faith is "made mature" as we do the work God directs us to perform (as taught by my wife Judith Peart).

[260] Hebrews 11:19

[261] Genesis 22:1-14

[262] Romans 4:13

[263] The Greek word "te" means "both" and "also."

[264] John 5:28

[265] Revelation 20:5-6

[266] Luke 14:14

[267] Matthew 22:31-32

[268] Matthew 13:37

[269] 1 Corinthians 15:38

[270] 1 Corinthians 15:24
[271] 1 Corinthians 15:24-26
[272] John 5:29, 2 Corinthians 5:10, Mark 3:28-29 w/Mark 3:22-27
[273] John 5:29
[274] 1 Corinthians 3:15
[275] Hebrews 5:9
[276] Revelation 3:5
[277] 1 Corinthians 3:15
[278] Numbers 21:14
[279] 2 Timothy 2:3-4
[280] James 2:21, 22, 24
[281] Malachi 3:16
[282] Isaiah 34:16
[283] Hebrews 10:7
[284] John 1:14
[285] 2 Corinthians 3:3
[286] 1 Corinthians 6:1-3
[287] 2 Corinthians 3:3
[288] 2 Corinthians 3:2
[289] Matthew 25:41
[290] 1 Corinthians 6:2-3
[291] 1 Corinthians 6:4 w/1 Corinthians 6:1-3
[292] Revelation 20:10; 20:14, Matthew 25:41
[293] 1 John 5:16
[294] 1 John 5:16 w/Revelation 20:14
[295] "World" in this verse (both places) is defined as "age."
[296] John 424
[297] 1 John 5:6
[298] Pharisees and Sadducees are also examples of religious leaders of today who say that speaking in tongues is evil, those who do not believe that saints can be filled with the Holy Spirit today, and so on.
[299] Please note the Scripture never said that Jesus would come "for" the Saints. The Scripture does say that Jesus would come "in" His saints and "with" His Saints.
[300] 1 John 3:22; 5:3
[301] 1 John 4:7-8
[302] 1 Corinthians 13
[303] Galatians 3:8-9
[304] Ezekiel 33:11

[305] 1 Timothy 2:4

[306] Matthew 25:31-32

[307] Revelation 19:20

[308] 1 John 4:18

[309] Luke 16:19-31

[310] Luke 14:14

[311] Romans 14:10 (future tense); 2 Corinthians 5:10 (aorist tense)

[312] Aorist tense means that there is no reference to time, duration, or repetition.

[313] Revelation 3:21

[314] The use of "cherubim of **glory**" in Hebrews 9:5 are called "cherubim of **gold**" in Exodus 25:18; therefore "gold" is a picture or symbol of God's "glory." According to 2 Chronicles 3:6, gold is also a symbol of bearing fruits (being fruitful).

[315] Hebrews 9:28

[316] Matthew 5:35; Acts 7:49; Isaiah 66:1

[317] 2 Chronicles 9:18a

[318] John 1:29; 1:36

[319] 1 Corinthians 4:4-5

[320] Hebrews 9:28; "the second time" is literally "out of the Second;" this "Second" in Hebrews 9:28 is the same "Second" in Hebrews 9:3 called the "Holiest of All (or Holy of Holies, or Most Holy Place);" the same "Second Part" in Hebrews 9:7, etc.; please read Hebrews 9:2-3; 9:6-7; 10:9; 9:28; and also see an Interlinear Bible for original/literal Greek rendering of Hebrews 9:28.

[321] Hebrews 10:16-18

[322] Hebrews 12:14

[323] Romans 2:29

[324] See Zep 3:16-17

[325] 1 John 1:9

[326] Acts 2:34-36 w/Revelation 3:21; Matthew 2:2 (Jesus "is born King.")

[327] 1 Corinthians 15:24-28

Appendix
Other Books by Donald and Judith Peart

Poiema, by Judith Peart
Wisdom from Above, by Judith Peart
Procreation, Understanding Sex, and Identity, by Judith Peart
100 Nevers, by Judith Peart
The Shattered and the Healing by Judith Peart
The Lamb, by Donald Peart
Jesus' Resurrection, Our Inheritance, by Donald Peart.
Sexuality, By Donald Peart
Forgiven 490, by Donald Peart w/Judith Peart!
The Days of the Seventh Angel, By Donald Peart
The Torah (The Principle) of Giving, by Donald Peart
The Time Came, by Donald Peart
The Last Hour, the First Hour, the Forty-Second Generation, by Donald Peart
Vision Real, by Donald Peart
The False Prophet, Alias, Another Beast V1, by Donald Peart
"the beast," by Donald Peart
Son of Man Prophesy Against the false prophet, by Donald Peart
The Dragon's Tail, the Prophets who Teach Lies, by Donald Peart
The Work of Lawlessness Revealed, by Donald Peart
When the Lord Made the Tempter, by Donald Peart
Examining Doctrine, Volume 1, by Donald Peart
Exousia, Your God Given Authority, by Donald Peart
The Numbers of God, by Donald Peart
The Completions of the Ages … by Donald Peart
The Revelation of Jesus Christ, by Donald Peart
Jude—Translation and Commentary, by Donald Peart
Obtaining the Better Resurrection, by Donald Peart
Manifestations from Our Lord Jesus …by Donald and Judith Peart).
Obtaining the Better Resurrection, by Donald Peart
The New Testament, Dr. Donald Peart Exegesis
The Tree of Life, By Dr. Donald Peart

Appendix
Other Books by Donald and Judith Peart

The Spirit and Power of John, the Baptist by Dr. Donald Peart
The Shattered and the Healing by Judith Peart
Is She Married to a Husband? by Donald Peart
The Ugliest Man God Made by Donald Peart
Does Answering the Call of God Impact Your Children? by Donald Peart
Victory Out-of-the Beast-the Harvest of the Earth by Donald Peart
Ezekiel-the House-the City-the Land (Interpreting the Patterns), by Donald Peart

Contact Information:

Crown of Glory Ministries
P.O. Box 1041 Randallstown, MD 21133
donaldpeart7@gmail.com

About the Author

Donald Peart is married to Judith Peart. Donald committed his life (though for a short period) while Judith recommitted her life to the Lord Jesus around the summer of 1981 after the pair kept reading the book of John and the book of Revelation. Donald read the entire book of Revelation and became especially interested in Revelation 20:4. Eventually, in April 1986, Donald and Judith permanently recommitted their lives to the Lord Jesus. They have been serving the Lord Jesus since and declaring the well-message of Jesus, the Christ. Over the years, the Lord Jesus has worked various manifestations of signs, wonders, and miracles through them. Below are three examples of the Lord Jesus' involvement in the lives of Donald and Judith.

In 1988, while living in North Carolina, the voice of the Lord spoke to Donald and said, "I have not called you to be an apostle, pastor, evangelist, teacher, but a ...(Donald blocked out the rest of the words the Lord was speaking to Him; because at the time, Donald was afraid God would call him to function in a ministry contrary to what Donald believed he should be functioning as--a prophet)." Approximately seventeen years later, on February 6, 2005, in Maryland, while Donald was on a fast; on the 13th day of the fast, the Lord Jesus resumed the conversation he had with Donald in 1988. As Donald listened, the voice of the Lord continued exactly as He spoke in 1988, "I have not called you to be a prophet, an apostle, an evangelist, a pastor, or teacher, but I have called you to be a son."

In 1990, while in prayer speaking to the heavenly Father about going to university to study engineering, Donald heard the

Lord Jesus say to him "you are as Joseph before me; go to engineering school; you will be good at it." The Lord also said to Donald, "this is the sign that I have spoken to you; your wife is pregnant with a girl." Donald responded to the Lord saying, "Joseph did not have any daughters." To which the Lord replied, "Joseph is a fruitful son, a fruitful son by a well whose daughters run over the wall." Donald immediately searched the Scriptures to see if Joseph had any daughters. The Scriptures confirmed that what the Lord spoke to Donald was correct. Genesis 49:22, translated from the Hebrew, states "Joseph is a fruitful son, a fruitful son by a well whose daughters run over the wall." The "sign" the Lord gave to Donald was fulfilled immediately. Judith Peart was already pregnant with their third child; a girl named Charity was born to them according to the time of life. Donald also graduated from engineering school. In addition to their five natural children, they have spiritual "daughters" and "sons " because God is fulfilling His word to them. This was also the second and third time the Lord called Donald a son.

On a day around 1991, Donald became disheartened, and he spoke to the Lord about his circumstances. At the time, he and his wife were experiencing extreme trials after Donald's obedience to the Lord. Donald was instructed to study God's Word exclusively, which turned out to be almost four years of intense study and prayer coupled with a time of consistent acute trials or probe-testing. As Donald sat on the sofa that day reading Genesis 2, the Lord began unveiling to Donald an understanding of Genesis 2 with an understanding he had not heard the elders teach. The Spirit of the Lord began to show Donald the sequence of creation, including the man (Adam), the original serpent, and Mrs. Adam (later called Eve). As the Spirit of Jesus revealed to Donald how the Scriptures in

Genesis 2 should be interpreted, his mind began questioning what he was reading and hearing in the Spirit. His mind questioned the revelation of the Holy Spirit due to previous doctrines he learned in church from the elders and commentaries. As Donald questioned the understanding the Spirit of God revealed to him, Donald saw the pages of the Bible he was reading being closed one by one, yet the physical Bible in his lap was still opened to the same pages he was reading. This is when he realized he was seeing a vision. The Lord then said to him, "Do not filter My Word through what the elders have taught you."

As a result of the Lord making Himself know to Donald and Judith throughout the years and providing explicit directions to Donald with regards God's doctrine, Donald and Judith have preached the gospel of Christ as the Lord has taught him; a gospel that is centered on Jesus Christ, the Son of the living God and the bride of Christ. With that said, the Lord Jesus has also graced Donald Peart to earn diplomas from Baltimore Polytechnic High School; an Associate of Arts degree in Pre-Engineering, a Bachelor of Science degree in Civil Engineering, a Master of Divinity, a Master of Science in Construction Management, and a Doctorate in Theology.

* 9 7 8 0 9 8 5 2 4 8 1 1 6 *